Law Es

COMPANY LAW

Josephine Bisacre, LL.B., LL.M.
Solicitor;
Senior Teaching Fellow in Business Law,
Heriot Watt University

and

Claire McFadzean, B.A.(Hons), LL.B., Dip. L.P.
Solicitor;
Lecturer in Law,
Glasgow Caledonian University

DUNDEE UNIVERSITY PRESS
2011

Published in Great Britain in 2011 by
Dundee University Press
University of Dundee
Dundee DD1 4HN

www.dundee.ac.uk/dup

ISBN 978–1–84586–080–6

No natural forests were destroyed to make this product;
only farmed timber was used and replanted

British Library Cataloguing-in-Publication data
A catalogue for this book is available on request from the British Library.

Typeset by Waverley Typesetters, Warham
Printed and bound by CPI Group (UK) Ltd, Croydon, CR0 4YY

CONTENTS

TABLE OF CASES

TABLE OF STATUTES

1 AGENCY

TRIPARTITE RELATIONSHIP

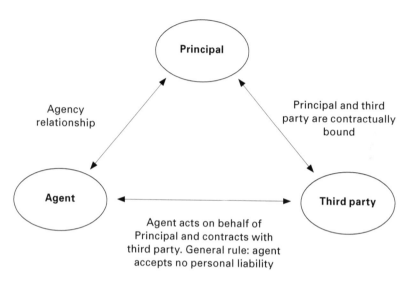

Figure 1.1: Tripartite relationship in agency

An agency relationship is a fiduciary relationship that exists between two parties. One party (the principal) expressly or impliedly consents that the other party (the agent) should act on his behalf and the agent must agree to act on the principal's behalf (see Figure 1.1). In entering into an agency relationship, the principal is allowing the agent contractually to affect his relations with third parties. Consequently, the key requirements are that a principal must bestow power on the agent to act on their behalf, and an agent must act within their requisite authority.

How do you know whether an agency relationship exists? Sometimes it can be established simply from the nature of the position a person holds, for example a director in a company (see Figure 1.2).

If it is not clear if an agency relationship exists, the courts may determine from the facts of the situation whether an agency relationship exists. This is regardless of whether the parties themselves would describe their relationship as one of agency. The courts look at each individual set of facts and circumstances and make a decision.

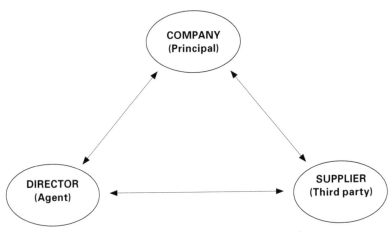

Figure 1.2: Agency relationship involving a company director

TYPES OF AGENT

General agents

A general agent is a person who has the authority to carry out all the ordinary commercial business on behalf of the principal (or all the business of a certain type). Third parties dealing with this type of agent can assume that they have a general continuing authority to act on behalf of the principal and that they have all the powers usually associated with an agent possessing such authority. Examples of general agents would be partners and directors.

Special agents

Special agents are appointed to carry out one particular transaction, therefore they do not have a continuing relationship with the principal. A special agent has implied powers only to the extent necessary to carry out the single transaction for which they have been appointed. An example of this would be an estate agent – they have the implied power necessary and associated with the ordinary commercial activity of selling a house.

HOW IS AN AGENCY RELATIONSHIP CREATED?

Expressly

An agency relationship can be established either in writing or orally. The discussion and ultimate agreement between the principal (to appoint) and the agent (acceptance of the terms of the relationship) would form a binding contract.

Impliedly

The agency relationship is implied by the nature of the appointment (by the principal) of the agent. For example, a partner is deemed an agent of the partnership by virtue of his appointment. In addition, the appointment of an employee to a senior or supervisory position within an organisation can often be perceived by a third party as implying that they have the authority to act as an agent for their employer (principal). In *Neville v C & A Modes* (1945) it was held that the manager of a shop had the implied authority to protect the owner's property against shoplifters. Furthermore, while it is possible to create an agency relationship by implication, the implication may cease due to a change in circumstances or by lapse of time.

"Holding out"

An agency relationship may be created where a person allows someone to represent themselves as their agent without objecting to such a representation. As a result, a third party may enter into contractual relations after reasonably relying on their actings.

Consequently, any principal who allows this representation to continue without objection cannot later deny that an agency relationship exists. This is primarily in order to protect the interests of third parties. In the case of *Freeman & Lockyer (A Firm) v Buckhurst Park Properties (Mangal) Ltd and Another* (1964) Mr Kapoor and Mr Hoon set up a private limited company, Buckhurst Park Properties (Mangal) Ltd ("the Company") and subscribed in equal shares. Both gentlemen were appointed as the Company's first directors along with a nominee of each. The business objective of the Company was to purchase Buckhurst Park Estate for £75,000, renovate and resell it.

While the Articles of Association ("the Articles") of the Company allowed for the appointment of a managing director, this was not formally done. Despite this, Mr Kapoor took the lead in dealing with the purchase and development of the estate, as Mr Hoon spent much of his time out of the country. Mr Kapoor instructed Freeman and Lockyer ("the Architects") to apply for planning permission in relation to the redevelopment of the estate. There was no dispute in this case as to quantum, simply whether it was the Company or Mr Kapoor who was liable under the contract. The Company argued that Mr Kapoor did not have authority to bind the Company and that he was personally liable. The Court of Appeal held that the Company was liable to pay the Architects. While Mr Kapoor did not have actual authority to bind the Company he did have ostensible authority, given that he acted as the managing director with the full knowledge of the board. In circumstances where an agent does not have actual authority to act, a third party can enforce a contract against the principal, if the following conditions are satisfied (Lord Diplock LJ at 506):

(i) "a representation that the agent had authority to enter on behalf of the company into a contract of the kind sought to be enforced …"

Mr Kapoor acted with the full knowledge of the board of directors, they did not attempt to intervene.

(ii) "that such a representation was made by a person or persons who had 'actual' authority to manage the business of the company …"

The Articles gave full power to the board of directors to manage the Company.

(iii) "that the [Architect] was induced by such representation to enter into the contract, that is, that he in fact relied upon it."

The Architects relied on Mr Kapoor's authority to bind the Company and the Architects at the relevant time believed that they were contracting with the Company.

(iv) "that under its memorandum and articles of association that company was not deprived of the capacity either to enter into a contract of the kind sought to be enforced or to delegate authority to enter into a contract of that kind to the agent".

The Articles of the Company allowed delegation of power to a managing director, although Mr Kapoor was not formally appointed as one. It is important to note that now, pursuant to s 40 of the Companies Act 2006, this point is largely redundant, provided that the third party acts in good faith.

Ratification

Ordinarily an agency relationship is constituted before an agent undertakes any actions on a principal's behalf. However, on occasion the sequence of events may be different. See Figure 1.3. It is possible for

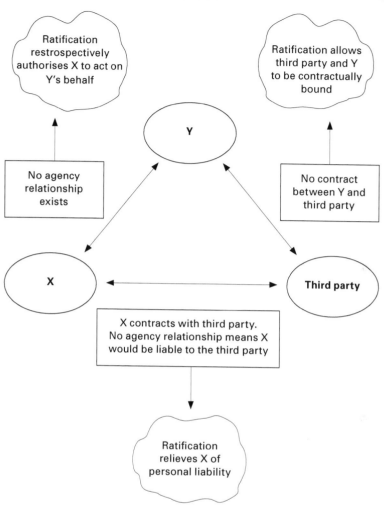

Figure 1.3: Ratification

one person (X) to act on behalf of a second person (Y) without prior authority. X may be treated as acting as the agent of Y if Y subsequently ratifies their actions. Ratification by Y may be express, implied or inferred from their conduct.

The effect of ratification is that it endorses the actions of X and gives them full validity and effect, as though it had been endorsed by Y from the time of X's action. Essentially, it is retrospective in effect. Consequently, if a third party contracts with X (and X's actions have been ratified by Y), then Y cannot withdraw from the contract with the third party.

There are a number of requirements in order for ratification to occur, including that the principal must have:

(i) existed at the time the contract was concluded between the agent and the third party (see Chapter 5 – case of *Tinnevelly*);

(ii) legal capacity to enter into the relevant contract; and

(iii) ratified the agent's actions timeously (*Goodall* v *Bisland* (1909)).

Necessity (or *negotiorum gestio*)

The creation of an agency relationship through necessity is today quite uncommon, not least of all because of the extensive modes of communication which are now widely available. Nowadays, it is perhaps more likely to occur if the individual is too medically incapacitated to issue instructions (*Fernie* v *Roberson* (1871)), thereby forcing another to take reasonable action on their behalf.

AN AGENT'S AUTHORITY TO ACT ON BEHALF OF A PRINCIPAL

It is imperative to ascertain whether an agent has the requisite authority to act on behalf of the principal as an agent's authority determines whether their actions are valid. In essence, it affects the legal relationship between agent, principal and third party.

The four types of authority which will be considered in turn are express, implied, ostensible and presumed authority. Express and implied authority may be described as actual authority arising from a contractual relationship, whereas ostensible and presumed authority could be categorised as authority which arises by operation of law.

Express authority

The agent's authority is expressly stated in an agreement between the principal and agent either in writing (this tends to be strictly construed by the courts) or orally. The third party at the time of negotiation with the agent may or may not have been aware of the agreement that existed between principal and agent. Despite the third party's lack of knowledge (at the requisite time), the third party nonetheless is entitled to rely upon the express authority whenever they become aware of it. Thus it is possible for a third party to ultimately establish a contractual relationship with the principal.

Where an agent exceeds the express authority bestowed by the principal and a third party is unable to rely upon any other form of authority or indeed subsequent ratification by the principal, ordinarily the principal is not bound by the agent's actions. Generally, the third party's right of recourse would be to proceed against the agent for having exceeded his authority.

Implied authority

An agent's authority may not be solely based on express authority; it may also be augmented by implied authority. Implied authority would allow an agent to do all that is necessary to discharge their duty in terms of the express agreement entered into with the principal.

Implied authority may arise from various factors such as the nature of the agent's appointment, the type of agent appointed and the surrounding circumstances of their appointment. The courts have created a number of presumptions against implied authority which include to borrow money, or to facilitate an overdraft on behalf of the principal. Ultimately, their actions must still flow from the contractual relationship.

Ostensible authority

In order for the principal to be bound by the actions of their agent, the agent must act within the authority bestowed upon them. However, it is not always the case that the requisite authority can be derived from a contractual arrangement. If it can be established that an agent has ostensible authority to act, the principal may then be contractually bound to a third party, despite the evident lack of actual authority.

The existence of ostensible authority may be established on the basis of actions of both principal and agent. The requirements include the following:

- the principal has in some way represented to a third party that the agent has authority to act; and
- the third party's belief that the agent has authority to act is based on the principal's representations. Clearly, if the third party knows the agent has no authority (or the third party knows the agent is acting in their own interest), irrespective of representations by the principal to the contrary, no ostensible authority can be established.

In the case of *International Sponge Importers Ltd* v *Andrew Watt & Sons* (1911), Mr Cohen was a travelling salesman ("the Agent") for International Sponge Importers Ltd ("the Principal"). The Agent had called on Messrs Watt ("Watt") for a number of years and would deliver sponges and collect payment by crossed cheque, payable to the Principal, all of which was within his authority. On four occasions, over a period of several years, the Agent induced Watt to pay for the sponges either by open cheque payable to him personally, or in cash. The Agent then embezzled the money. The Principal brought an action against Watt for payment in respect of the sponges delivered by the Agent.

The court held that all the payments made by Watt were valid and consequently Watt had settled their account in respect of the sponges. A key factor in the court's decision was that Watt had been acting in good faith, believing that the Agent had authority to receive payment by open cheque or by cash. Watt's integrity was indisputable and this method of payment had been brought to the Principal's attention in the past and was permitted to continue.

In *International Sponge Importers Ltd*, the conclusion that the Agent did possess ostensible authority to act on behalf of the Principal was primarily based on the Principal's previous conduct. Often the issue of authority becomes a matter of contention, where contractual authority has been altered or indeed withdrawn from the agent. In this situation, the principal should notify all third parties who have had prior dealings with the agent, in order to protect themselves from any potential liability in future contracts.

Clearly, it is often in a third party's interest to establish ostensible authority, given the protection it affords them. It should be noted that where a third party is successful in this endeavour, the agent remains unauthorised to act on the principal's behalf. However, by establishing ostensible authority it prevents the principal relying on an agent's lack of authority in order to avoid the concluded contract.

Presumed authority

Where there is lack of authority, the courts may presume that the necessary authority would have been forthcoming, if the agent had been able to contact the principal, for example where an emergency occurs. It is important to note that the conferring of presumed authority is on the decrease as there are now such widespread methods of communication available.

DUTIES OWED BY AN AGENT

Agents owe a variety of duties to their principals, including the following:

Acting in person (*delegatus non potest delegare*)

When a principal appoints an agent, the individual's character, qualities and experience often play a crucial role in their decision. Therefore, the general rule is that it is not acceptable for an agent to delegate their responsibilities to someone else. However, in circumstances where the principal authorises such a delegation, or where it would be considered normal practice, in a particular trade or profession, it is permissible to deviate from this rule (*Cornelius* v *Black* (1897)).

Following instructions

Where a principal provides an agent with explicit instructions which are lawful and reasonable, an agent has a duty to comply. Failure to comply may result in the agent being personally liable for any losses incurred by the principal. Should the principal's instructions not be clear, an agent may not be held liable for misconstruing them.

Acting in good faith

The relationship between agent and principal can be described as fiduciary in nature. An agent should always be acting in the interests of the principal. However, should an agent act in their own interest or in the interests of another principal, it does not automatically mean they have breached their duty to act in good faith (*Lothian* v *Jenolite Ltd* (1969)). While an agent is not prohibited from acting for more than one principal (although it can be expressly prohibited in the agency agreement), they are opening themselves up to the possibility of conflicts of interest and the risk of prejudicing one principal for the benefit of another (*Liverpool Victoria Friendly Society* v *Houston* (1900)).

There is no comprehensive list of requirements that an agent must adhere to in order to successfully discharge their duty to act in good faith. Nevertheless, an agent should always maintain a principal's confidentiality (even after cessation of the agency relationship), and ought not to sell to, or purchase from, a principal without the principal being fully aware of the parties to the contract. Furthermore, an agent should not retain any financial benefit derived from a transaction where they are acting on behalf of the principal. If the principal subsequently discovers the benefit enjoyed by the agent they may, *inter alia*, terminate the agency relationship.

Exercising reasonable care and skill

When discharging their duties, an agent must always exercise reasonable care and skill to the standards expected by the ordinary "prudent man" (Bell, *Commentaries*, I, 516) or of the standards expected by their profession (which is often higher). Provided the agent has complied with the principal's explicit instructions and met the requisite standard of care and skill, the agent will not be in breach of duty. Where the principal has given the agent an element of discretion when acting on their behalf, the agent will not be liable for any losses suffered by the principal provided they have acted reasonably when exercising this discretion.

Accounting to the principal for funds received

When an agent is acting on behalf of a principal, it is commonplace for the agent to come into receipt of funds, which they hold on behalf of the principal. Should there be any deficit in these funds (for any reason) the agent must recompense the principal. In *Tyler* v *Logan* (1904), following a stock take in a boot shop, it came to light there was a shortfall. Despite there being no suggestion of dishonesty or negligence on the part of the shop manager, he was nonetheless held liable to compensate his employer (the principal). The stock was under his care and he was responsible for managing it.

This duty extends to providing the principal with all benefits derived from a transaction, including any interest earned on funds received by an agent and discounts enjoyed on a transaction. However, an agent is under no obligation to provide funds to a principal until they are in receipt of cleared funds.

RIGHTS ENJOYED BY AN AGENT

Remuneration

Ordinarily, an agent will receive remuneration for the services they provide on behalf of a principal. Generally, this will be set out expressly in a contract but it may be provided for in an alternative manner: for example, it can be calculated based on an hourly rate.

Remuneration only becomes payable by a principal when an agent fulfils the obligations which entitle payment. It is not necessarily a requirement that a principal has actually benefited from the agent's endeavours (*Dudley Bros & Co* v *Barnet* (1937)).

Indemnification

An agent's right to be indemnified by a principal may be expressly or impliedly part of their agency contract. The extent of indemnification will vary depending on the kind of business the principal is involved in. The relief may be granted in respect of any expenses, liabilities and losses an agent properly incurs in the exercise of their duties provided, *inter alia*, they have not acted outwith their authority or in breach of their fiduciary duties.

Lien

Where a principal has failed to indemnify an agent or pay their agreed remuneration (or commission), an agent has the right of lien over all property of the principal rightly in their possession:

- *General lien* – applies only to a limited number of agents, including solicitors, and allows such an agent to hold onto any property of the principal. It does not necessarily have to directly relate to their debt: eg a corporate solicitor may hold onto completion documents until the principal settles a debt owed to a colleague in another department.

- *Special lien* – this type of lien applies to the vast majority of agents and requires that only property relating to the specific debt may be held by the agent until settlement.

CONTRACTING WITH DISCLOSED OR UNDISCLOSED PRINCIPALS – DOES IT MAKE A DIFFERENCE?

Certain distinctions may be made where a third party is contracting with an agent and the existence of a principal is disclosed (named or unnamed) or where the third party is unaware of the existence of an agency relationship.

Disclosed and named principal

Ordinarily, where an agent discloses the existence of an agency relationship to a third party and names the principal, the contract negotiated by the agent will be binding on the third party and the principal. Generally, in such circumstances the agent will not be held liable for any subsequent breach of contract. Exceptions to this rule include where it would be accepted in a particular trade or profession that an agent would assume personal liability pursuant to a contract: eg firms of solicitors (as agents for their clients) regularly accept personal liability by granting a letter of obligation in a conveyancing transaction (*Johnston v Little* (1960)).

Disclosed and unnamed principal

Generally, the position is the same as a disclosed and named principal, although it should be noted that there is very little Scottish authority on this issue. Common law provides some guidance although unfortunately it does not provide absolute clarity.

Often for the courts the pivotal question is, at the time of contracting, was it the principal's credit or the agent's credit that the third party was relying upon. Another approach is to consider the "doctrine of election". In the case of *Ferrier* v *Dods* (1865), the agent (an auctioneer) was selling a horse on behalf of an unnamed principal (owner of the horse). Following completion of the sale, the purchaser was dissatisfied with the horse and, once they had identified the principal, proceeded to return the horse to them. The court held that this was an acceptable course of action. The third party had a right of recourse against both principal and agent and had "elected" to pursue the principal.

Clearly, if the identity of the principal is not known (or cannot be easily ascertained) the doctrine of election is not applicable. The only remedy available to the third party is against the agent as they have been denied any alternative course of action.

Undisclosed principal

When a third party is contracting with an agent they may be unaware of the existence of an agency relationship. The general rule is that both (undisclosed) principal and agent may be held liable for any subsequent breach of contract, by the third party. In this scenario the agent has potentially opened themselves up to personal liability, as the third party does not know of the existence of the principal and believes they have entered into a contract with the agent.

Following execution of the contract, the agent may then disclose the principal's existence to the third party. Where this occurs the principal may then gain rights against the third party (*Bennett* v *Inveresk Paper Co*

(1891)) and vice versa. If the third party has grounds to sue on the contract they must choose to pursue either the principal or the agent. However, once they have elected whom they intend to hold liable, the decision is final (discussed above – see *Ferrier*), and they cannot at a later date pursue the other party.

WHAT IS AN AGENT'S LIABILITY WHEN THEY EXCEED THEIR AUTHORITY?

In order for an agent to successfully bind a principal they must contract within the scope of the authority conferred upon them. If they exceed their authority, then they may open themselves up to personal liability.

The remedies available to a third party where an agent has exceeded their authority and the principal has not opted to ratify the agent's actions include:

- a delictual action for damages where the agent has acted fraudulently or negligently; or
- a contractual action for breach of warranty (the third party must have relied on the representation made by the agent and as a result suffered a loss).

TERMINATION OF THE AGENCY RELATIONSHIP

An agency relationship may be brought to an end in a variety of ways. They can be broadly categorised as follows.

By actions of principal and/or agent

This would include the following:

- both principal and agent mutually agree to bring their agency relationship to an end;
- one party gives notice to the other of their intention to terminate the agency relationship; or
- there is a trigger of a termination clause within their agency contract.

In some circumstances it is prudent for a principal to notify third parties that the agent no longer has any authority to act on their behalf, thus preventing the agent from further binding the principal in future transactions. In addition, general notice can be given to the public at large by publishing a notice in the *Edinburgh Gazette* (Partnership Act 1890, s 36).

By operation of law

This would include the following:

- death of the agent or principal;
- impossibility or illegality;
- bankruptcy or liquidation; or
- frustration.

Essential Facts

- An agency relationship is a fiduciary relationship that exists between two parties, namely the principal and the agent.
- An agency relationship may be created either expressly, impliedly, by "holding out", ratification or through necessity.
- In order to bind the principal to a third party an agent must have requisite authority to act. Authority may be bestowed expressly, impliedly, ostensibly or can be presumed.
- Agents owe a number of duties (eg to act in person and to exercise reasonable care and skill) to the principal, as well as enjoying a number of rights (including remuneration, indemnification and lien).
- Termination of the agency relationship may occur either by the actions of the principal and/or agent or by operation of law.

Essential Cases

Freeman & Lockyer (A Firm) v Buckhurst Park Properties (Mangal) Ltd and Another (1964): an agency relationship may be created in circumstances where a person allows someone to represent themselves as an agent. It was held in this case that the principal cannot later deny the existence of the agency relationship where this occurs, and the third party was entitled to payment by the principal.

International Sponge Importers Ltd v Andrew Watt & Sons (1911): the existence of ostensible authority may be established by the previous actions of the principal. An important factor in this case was that the third party was acting in good faith at all times and believed that the agent had the requisite authority.

Ferrier v Dods (1865): considers the "doctrine of election". Where a principal is disclosed but unnamed, at the point of conclusion of the contract, the third party has a right of redress against both principal and agent and must "elect" who to pursue.

2 PARTNERSHIPS

The Partnership Act 1890 (the "1890 Act") established the foundations of partnership law. Where no formal partnership agreement is entered into, disputes or misunderstandings between the partners will be resolved based on the provisions of the 1890 Act. From both a practical and a commercial point of view, it is always advisable to reduce any agreement to writing.

The formation of a partnership is not subject to the same stringent formalities as other business vehicles and it can be created verbally or be inferred by the conduct of the parties. In order for a partnership to exist, the individuals must have come together in order to carry on a business (1890 Act, s 45) with a view to making a profit (1890 Act, s 1(1)).

Partnerships in Scotland are seen as having a quasi-legal personality. They are distinct from their partners, therefore a partnership is able to enter into contracts, sue and be sued. However, partners are agents and guarantors of the partnership and are consequently jointly and severally liable for the debts and obligations of the partnership (1890 Act, s 9).

FORMATION OF A PARTNERSHIP

The minimum number of partners required to form a partnership is two and there is now no statutory maximum number of partners. Each person must have capacity to be a partner in a firm, and this would include being of sound mind and sufficient age. Furthermore, where a partnership has been formed with the intention of carrying on an illegal business, any partnership agreement will be deemed void. In circumstances where a partnership fails to comply with all the statutory requirements, it will leave each of the partners open to unlimited personal liability in respect of all debts incurred by the firm.

In circumstances where a firm uses a trading name (instead of the surnames of the partners) common law ensures that the firm does not use a name which is the same or similar to an existing firm's name (this is in order to prevent third-party confusion). Where a firm ignores this duty, it may result in an interdict being sought on the basis of "passing off". In addition, the Companies Act 2006 provides some additional parameters in terms of a firm's name.

TYPES OF PARTNERS

There are a number of different types of partners that may exist within a firm. They include the following.

General

A general partner is one who is actively involved in the daily management of the firm and who is responsible for making business decisions. The rights this type of partner enjoys may vary within a partnership agreement. However, if no such agreement is executed then s 24 of the 1890 Act provides guidance on their rights (discussed below).

Limited

A limited partner enjoys limited liability in terms of a partnership's debts. Given that, ordinarily, partners are jointly and severally liable for the debts of a firm, there is additional regulation governing this type of partnership in terms of the Limited Partnerships Act 1907 (discussed below).

Sleeping

While the term "sleeping partners" is widely used, it is not a legal term as such. It is accepted that this type of partner will not be involved in the daily management or decision-making process of a partnership. Despite this, a sleeping partner for other purposes is treated similarly to a general partner; they share equally in the profits and losses of the partnership (1890 Act, s 24).

Salaried

It is common practice for some professional partnerships (eg firms of solicitors) to have salaried partners. This type of partner is represented as a partner of the firm on its correspondence and they are equally liable for the partnership's debts. However, they do not receive an equal share of the partnership's profits; rather, they receive a salary.

CONTRACTING WITH THIRD PARTIES

In the ordinary course of business it is unlikely that third parties will have any knowledge of the specific authority bestowed on an individual partner of a firm. Given that a partner can be described as an agent of the firm, partners can contractually bind the firm by any acts carried on in the ordinary course of the firm's business (1890 Act, s 5). Furthermore, where a partner has authority bestowed upon him to act on behalf of the firm, and he does so in the firm's name, he is able to bind the partnership and his fellow partners in relation to third-party contracts. In the case of *Mercantile Credit Co Ltd v Garrod* (1962), the firm had entered into a partnership agreement regulating the type of work it would undertake. It expressly stated it would not be involved in the buying and selling of cars. In contravention of this, one of the partners sold a car. The court held the firm was liable under the contract, as it was the type of business a third party (acting in good faith) would believe the firm would be involved in and this was the significant factor, not what the partners had agreed between themselves.

A partner's authority can be restricted by a firm (eg within a partnership agreement). Where a third party is unaware of the restriction, they can rely on the implied or ostensible authority of a partner, when the contract concerns the ordinary business of a firm (1890 Act, s 5). In circumstances where a partner attempts contractually to bind a firm in a transaction outwith the scope of its normal business, the partnership will not be required to comply with the terms of the contract, unless the partner concerned had been given specific authority to contract (1890 Act, s 7). Where a third party knows or believes that a partner does not have authority, there is no valid contract, and the partner concerned is personally liable.

THE RIGHTS AND DUTIES OF PARTNERS

The relationship between partners and a firm can be described as fiduciary in nature. Sections 28–30 of the 1890 Act provide guidance on the type of duties owed by partners; these include a duty to provide accounts of the firm's business to any partner, to account to the partnership for any personal profits derived from any transactions concerning the firm, and a duty not to compete with the partnership's business.

The rights which partners enjoy can be agreed or indeed varied by the consent of all the partners (1890 Act, s 19). In the absence of any agreement between the partners as to their contractual rights, s 24 of the 1890 Act provides guidance, which includes:

- entitlement to an equal share of capital and profits of a firm;
- indemnification for any financial outlays or personal liabilities a partner incurs in the ordinary course of a firm's business; and
- a right both to be involved in management of the partnership's business, and to inspect the partnership books.

Partnerships do not have to rely on the 1890 Act for regulation. Partners have the capacity to enter into a partnership agreement, thereby agreeing between themselves how they want their own partnership to operate (1890 Act, s 19). However, the 1890 Act provides a ready source of guidance (1890 Act, ss 19–31) where there is a failure to execute a negotiated agreement (or the agreement is silent on a particular issue). The principles of the 1890 Act include the following.

Delectus personae

Partnerships may be described as a fiduciary relationship; therefore, every partner should be acting in good faith. Each partner must always act in the best interest of the firm, therefore should not make personal gain at the expense of the partnership (1890 Act, s 30) and should make full disclosure to their co-partners on matters affecting the firm.

Consequently, when setting up a partnership, or indeed inviting an individual to join an existing partnership, the personal qualities that the individual brings to the firm are of significant importance to their co-partners.

Partnership at will

Where a partnership is carrying on in business, and no fixed term has been prescribed for its existence, any partner at any time can give notice to all the other partners of their intention to end the partnership (1890 Act, s 26(1)).

Introduction of a new partner

No new partner may be introduced to the firm without the unanimous consent of all existing partners (1890 Act, s 24(7)).

Assignment of rights

Given that the choice of partner in a firm is of utmost importance, you cannot assign your partnership. Any assignment by a partner is only to the extent of their share of the profits (1890 Act, s 31(1)). An assignment does not entitle the assignee to interfere in the firm's business.

Expulsion of a partner

No majority of partners can decide to expel another partner from the firm (1890 Act, s 25), unless there is an express agreement conveying such power. In circumstances where there is a negotiated agreement which provides an expulsion clause, it can only be exercised in its strictest interpretation, following the procedure set out in the agreement, and it can only be implemented when it is in the best interest of the partnership to do so.

LIABILITIES

Incoming partners

The general rule is that an incoming partner is usually not liable for the pre-existing debts of a firm (1890 Act, s 17(1)). Circumstances where this would not occur include the execution of an agreement to the contrary (1890 Act, s 19) or where a new firm has been created (by a change in constitution) and the new firm has taken on the debts of the dissolved firm.

Retiring partners

Any partner who retires will remain liable for all the debts incurred by the partnership prior to his retiral (1890 Act, s 17(2)). In order to be freed from this obligation an express agreement must be entered into between the retiring partner, the firm and all relevant creditors (1890 Act, s 17(3)). It is important to note the agreement will not be binding if there is no creditor consent.

The general position following the date of retiral is that all debts incurred thereafter are the sole responsibility of the partnership, provided that the appropriate notice of the said retiral has been given. Third parties who have had prior dealings with the firm are entitled to receive personal notification detailing the change in its constitution (1890 Act, s 36(1)). It is clearly in the retiring partner's interest to provide this information expediently to avoid any contractual liability going forward. In circumstances where third parties have had no prior dealings with the partnership, it is acceptable to notify a change in its constitution by publishing a notice to that effect in the *Edinburgh Gazette* (1890 Act, s 36(2)).

"Holding out"

Under the 1890 Act, anyone who represents themself as a partner of a particular partnership, or indeed allows someone else to hold them out as a partner, may indeed be held liable in respect of any contractual arrangement that was entered into by a third party on the basis of that representation (1890 Act, s 14(1)). In the case of *Hosie* v *Waddell* (1866), Waddell, in reliance on a representation, paid money in settlement of a debt, to an individual they believed was Hosie's partner. The reality of the situation was that the individual was an employee, who subsequently absconded with the money. The court held that the debt had been duly settled, as the individual had been held out as a partner.

Delict

In circumstances where an individual (not including a partner in the firm) suffers a loss or injury as a direct result of "any wrongful act or omission of any partner acting in the ordinary course of the business of the firm, or with the authority of his co-partners" (1890 Act, s 10), the firm may be held liable to the same extent as the party guilty of the conduct (1890 Act, s 12).

If the firm is unable to meet this liability, each partner within the partnership is jointly and severally liable in delict to the injured third party (1890 Act, s 12). While all innocent partners have a right of redress against the guilty partner should they have to recompense the third party, financially, this right may be of little comfort. Arguably, if the guilty partner could have met the liability themself then the third party would not have been looking to the other partners for payment.

Liability of co-partners was considered in the case of *Kirkintilloch Equitable Co-operative Society* v *Livingstone* (1972). Richard Jackson was a chartered accountant and a partner in Hardie Cuthbertson & Co ("the Firm"). Jackson personally acted as official auditor for Kirkintilloch Equitable Co-operative Society ("Kirkintilloch") and he, not the Firm, was approved by the Treasury (in terms of the Industrial and Provident Societies Acts only individuals can be appointed auditors) to act in this capacity. Kirkintilloch raised an action against Jackson and his partners for damages, *inter alia*, on the grounds of negligence. The Firm was included in the action as it received payment for the audit and some employees of the Firm assisted Jackson with the audit. Kirkintilloch argued, on the basis of s 10 of the 1890 Act, that if the Firm was liable for Jackson's negligence, so too were his co-partners:

> "Where, by any wrongful act or omission of any partner acting in the ordinary course of the business of the firm, or with the authority of his co-partners, loss or injury is caused to any person not being a partner in the firm, or any penalty is incurred, the firm is liable therefor to the same extent as the partner so acting or omitting to act."

The Firm argued that the auditing of Kirkintilloch's accounts was not in their ordinary course of business, as the Firm could not legally be appointed as auditor. Consequently, Kirkintilloch's action was irrelevant and should be dismissed.

The court held that the Firm was liable for the losses as auditing of accounts would, *inter alia*, be within the ordinary scope of the Firm's business, and the fact that the Firm could not be appointed as official auditor does not detract from this fact.

DISSOLUTION

Partnerships may be dissolved for a variety of reasons. Circumstances which do not require a court order include:

- where a partnership was created for a fixed period of time or for a specific purpose, and the time has expired or the purpose has been achieved, the partnership naturally dissolves (1890 Act, s 32);
- automatic dissolution on death, bankruptcy (1890 Act, s 33) or resignation of a partner, unless an agreement has been made to the contrary; or
- where it would be unlawful for a partnership to continue in its business (1890 Act, s 34).

The 1890 Act provides a number of grounds where the court may intervene (1890 Act, s 35) and dissolve a partnership. This includes where:

- a partner is found to be permanently of unsound mind (1890 Act, s 35(a));
- a partner is guilty of persistently breaching the terms of the partnership agreement (1890 Act, s 35(d)); or
- the firm's business can only go forward by making a loss (1890 Act, s 35(e)).

Following the dissolution of a partnership, the partners typically have continued authority to wind up the firm's business (1890 Act, s 38). This can include completing any business the firm contractually undertook before the dissolution, since failure to do so may result in the partners being held professionally negligent. Once all the partnership's business has been concluded and debts settled, any surplus assets are shared among the partners (1890 Act, s 39).

CONSIDERING PARTNERSHIPS

A business vehicle's suitability will largely be dependent on an individual's business needs. When considering setting up a partnership, there are pros and cons, including the following.

Advantages

- No requirement to put documents into the public domain.
- Informal and flexible business vehicle.

Disadvantages

- Generally, partners have no personal protection against the financial liabilities of the partnership; therefore their personal assets may be at risk.
- Dissolution is often inevitable on the death of a partner or where a dispute arises between partners, which results in a partner's resignation.

LIMITED PARTNERSHIPS

Limited partnerships may be created under the Limited Partnership Act 1907 (as amended) (the "1907 Act"). Unless there is express provision to the contrary, limited partnerships will be governed in the same way as partnerships under the 1890 Act ("1890 Act") and common law.

Constitution

There are two types of partners in a limited partnership: general partners and limited partners. To constitute a limited partnership there must be a minimum of one general partner and one limited partner.

General partners

A general partner is unable to limit their liability in respect of the debts incurred by the firm. Consequently, they have unlimited liability should the firm be unable to honour the debts of its creditors (1907 Act, s 4(2)).

Limited partners

Limited partners enjoy the protection of limited liability in terms of the debts incurred by the limited partnership. The amount of their individual liability will be limited to the partner's capital contribution (1907 Act, s 4(2) and (3)).

There are numerous rules governing the relationship between general and limited partners (1907 Act, s 6(5)), including the following:

- the introduction of a new partner does not require consent of a limited partner (1907 Act, s 6(5)(d)); and
- a limited partner does not have authority to dissolve the partnership (1907 Act, s 6(5)(e)).

Registration and management

Unlike partnerships constituted under the 1890 Act, specific details of a limited partnership must be registered with the Registrar (1907 Act, s 8A) and the Registrar must be kept informed of any changes (1907 Act, s 9). Furthermore, when registering a limited partnership, the name must end with the words "limited partnership" or "LP" (1907 Act, s 8B(2)).

Limited partners must not involve themselves in the management of a limited partnership; if they do so, they will lose the protection of their limited status and be treated as general partners in terms of the financial liability to third parties (1907 Act, s 6(1)).

While they must not be involved in management, they (and their agents) are entitled to inspect partnership books and examine and advise on the direction and potential of the partnership (1907 Act, s 6(1)).

Dissolution and winding up

Generally, a limited partnership will not be dissolved by death or bankruptcy, or lunacy of a limited partner (1907 Act, s 6(2)). In circumstances where a limited partnership is dissolved, the winding-up process is ordinarily carried out by the general partner (1907 Act, s 6(3)), unless the court gives direction to the contrary.

Essential Facts

- Key legislation (partnerships) – the Partnership Act 1890.
- A partnership can be created with a minimum of two partners (no maximum limit) and have a quasi-legal personality.
- Entering into a partnership agreement is optional; however, it is possible to create a partnership both verbally or by inference based on the conduct of the parties.
- The relationship between the firm and its partners is fiduciary in nature.

- Partners are agents of a firm and can bind a partnership, and are jointly and severally liable.
- Partnerships can be dissolved for a variety of reasons, with or without a court order.
- Key legislation (limited partnerships) – Limited Partnerships Act 1907 (as amended).
- Constitution of limited partnership – a minimum of one general and one limited partner is required.
- The name of the limited partnership must end with the words "limited partnership" or "LP".
- Partners are under an obligation to notify certain information to the Registrar.

Essential Cases

Mercantile Credit Co Ltd v Garrod (1962): considers a contract entered into by a partner (on behalf of the firm) with a third party. The significance of this case is that a partnership can be held liable under this contract, if the type of business conducted is what a third party (acting in good faith) would assume to be in the ordinary course of the firm's business. This is regardless of any restriction that is imposed on a partner's authority to contract.

Kirkintilloch Equitable Co-operative Society v Livingstone (1972): considers the liability of co-partners; the negligence of a partner, while "acting in the ordinary course of the business of the firm" (1890 Act, s 10) rendered the firm liable for the losses suffered by the third party.

3 LIMITED LIABILITY PARTNERSHIPS

The Limited Liability Partnerships Act 2000 (as amended) ("2000 Act") introduced a new corporate vehicle to the world of business; the limited liability partnership ("LLP"). An LLP can be described as a hybrid vehicle, between a company limited by shares and a partnership.

SETTING UP AN LLP

As with the incorporation of a company, an LLP does not come into existence until all the necessary formalities of incorporation have been completed (2000 Act, s 2), and a certificate of incorporation has been issued by the Registrar.

In order to incorporate an LLP, an incorporation document (Form LL IN01) requires to be completed and sent to the Registrar with the requisite fee. Two or more individuals are required to be the initial members of an LLP and their names and addresses must be included on the incorporation document. A unique requirement of an LLP is the appointment of a minimum of two "designated members". Failure to adhere to this requirement results in all members being deemed to be "designated members" (2000 Act, s 2(2)(f)).

The role that "designated members" undertake cannot be found in any one piece of legislation. Their duties are largely administrative and are not dissimilar to the duties carried out by officers of a company. The 2000 Act provides guidance on the appointment and removal of designated members and the type of information that they must file with the Registrar.

In addition, the incorporation document requires a name to be chosen for an LLP that ends with the words "Limited Liability Partnership" or "LLP" (2000 Act, Sch 1, para 2) and it must not be the same name as any existing UK company or LLP (this can easily be checked online at Companies House). Additional restrictions on the name can be found in a number of amendments to the 2000 Act, including the Limited Liability Partnerships (Application of Companies Act) Regulations 2009 (SI 2009/1804) and the Company, Limited Liability Partnerships and Business Names (Sensitive Words and Expressions) Regulations 2009 (SI 2009/2615). A registered office must also be selected, and one of the subscribers or a solicitor involved in the incorporation of an LLP must acknowledge that the LLP is being set up to carry "on a lawful business with a view to profit" (2000 Act, s 2(1)(a)).

A membership agreement is not a requirement in order to incorporate an LLP, although it is advisable for members to regulate their relationship in advance of any issues arising. If no membership agreement is executed, the Limited Liability Partnerships Regulations 2001 (SI 2001/1090) ("2001 Regulations") provide guidance on how members' relationships with each other should be regulated. The 2001 Regulations are essentially default rules; however, they are not extensive and may not accurately reflect the intention of the members of an LLP, both in relation to its internal management and to its commercial objectives.

KEY FEATURES

An LLP is often described as a hybrid between a partnership and a limited liability company, given its mix of company and partnership features. Some of these features are detailed below.

Company features

- An LLP has a legal personality distinct from its members (2000 Act, s 1(1)); consequently, it enjoys perpetual succession. In addition, there is no limit to its capacity (2000 Act, s 1(3)), therefore the doctrine of *ultra vires* does not apply.
- The members of an LLP act as agents (2000 Act, s 6(1)) and, therefore, enjoy limited liability as do shareholders of a company.
- Members can bind an LLP, in a similar way to directors of a company, and as a result LLPs can own property, enter into contracts, sue and be sued. An LLP is also liable for its own debts, up to the value of the assets of an LLP, since members are not jointly liable.
- In order to offer a degree of protection to third parties, an LLP is under a statutory requirement to file documents with the Registrar: eg accounts and annual returns.
- Where a third party is contracting with an LLP, they can assume that a member has authority to act on its behalf. However, if they know that the member does not have such authority, or they know or believe that he is not a member of the LLP, then the LLP is not contractually bound by that member's actions. The assumption of membership can continue until notice of cessation has been intimated to the third party directly or to the Registrar (2000 Act, s 6(3)).

- Legislation, including the Companies Act 2006 and the Insolvency Act 1986 ("1986 Act"), applies to LLPs in a similar way to the manner in which it applies to companies. Consequently, members of LLPs (like company directors) have to be fully aware, *inter alia*, of how the provisions relating to wrongful and fraudulent trading, insolvency and disqualification may be applicable.

Partnership features

- An LLP does not have any directors, shareholders or share capital.

- Members' autonomy is similar to that enjoyed by partners. There is little regulation governing the internal management of an LLP, therefore members can choose how decisions should be made and profits shared, and how to regulate the appointment and retirement of members.

- A membership agreement is similar to a partnership agreement, in that it is optional (given that default provisions are provided by the 2001 Regulations) and there is no requirement to place the document in the public domain by filing it with the Registrar.

- Insolvency procedures for LLPs are very similar to those applicable to companies. However, the notable difference is that LLPs are subject to the "clawback" rule. This means that members have a very real personal interest in keeping abreast of the financial position of an LLP. In reality, if a member withdraws money from an LLP within 2 years prior to an insolvent winding up and knew, or ought to have known, that, given the withdrawal, an insolvent liquidation was unavoidable (1986 Act, s 214(2)(b)), the amount can be clawed back from that individual member. In this way members' personal exposure is similar to that of partners.

- LLPs enjoy similar tax transparency to partnerships. Generally, members will have the same income tax and corporation tax liabilities as partners and may enjoy similar benefits in relation to national insurance contributions.

CONSIDERING AN LLP

When considering incorporating an LLP, the positives and negatives associated with this type of business vehicle should be weighed up. They include the following.

Advantages

- Substantial protection of members' personal assets.
- Internal flexibility regarding management and structure.
- Tax transparency and benefits.

Disadvantages

- Limited financial privacy, given the filing requirements.
- It is a relatively new entity, therefore limited case law exists, and this perhaps gives a perception of legal uncertainty, and in turn may dissuade third parties from contracting with LLPs.

Essential Facts

- Legislation – the Limited Liability Partnerships Act 2000 (as amended) and the Limited Liability Partnerships Regulations 2001.
- An LLP can be described as a hybrid between a limited liability company and a partnership.
- An LLP is incorporated by sending an incorporation document to the Registrar, with the requisite fee.
- An LLP has a legal personality distinct from those of its members; therefore, it can hold property in its own name and enter into contracts.
- Members are agents of an LLP and therefore enjoy substantial limited liability.
- A membership agreement is optional, as default rules are provided by the 2001 Regulations.

4 TYPES OF COMPANIES

Private companies limited by shares are by far the most common type of company and will be the main focus of discussion. However, it is important to be aware that other types of companies also exist, including public companies, companies limited by guarantee and companies with unlimited liability.

PUBLIC COMPANIES

Any company that is not incorporated as a public limited company ("plc") will be deemed a private company, pursuant to s 4(1) of the Companies Act 2006 ("2006 Act"). There are a number of significant differences between a plc and a private limited company, including the following:

- A minimum share capital requirement exists for the setting up of a plc (2006 Act, ss 761(3) and 763), and the "authorised minimum" (2006 Act, s 763(1)) is £50,000 or Euro equivalent. (A difference has been eradicated by the 2006 Act, in that a plc no longer requires to have a minimum of two shareholders; now, like a private limited company, the minimum is one shareholder (2006 Act, Sch 16).)

- A plc requires a trading certificate before it can commence business (2006 Act, s 761). If the plc does not first obtain this certificate, the veil of incorporation will be lifted and the directors may be held jointly and severally liable (2006 Act, s 767(3)).

- There is a statutory requirement for a public company to have a minimum of two directors (2006 Act, s 154(2)), unlike a private limited company where the minimum number is one (2006 Act, s 154(1)).

- A directorship in a public company is comparatively more difficult to achieve: the process would usually involve a formal nomination procedure (2006 Act, s 160).

- The appointment of a company secretary is mandatory for a plc (2006 Act, s 271). They must possess the necessary qualifications and/or experience in order to discharge this office (2006 Act, s 273) (see Chapter 18).

- Plcs must hold an Annual General Meeting (2006 Act, s 336(1)). Private companies under the 2006 Act are now no longer obliged to do so, although they may opt in to this process.

COMPANIES LIMITED BY GUARANTEE

This type of company is very similar to a private company limited by shares; however, instead of a shareholder's liability being limited to the value of their shares, a member's liability will be limited to the amount which they guarantee (2006 Act, s 11). Often this type of company is used by charities.

UNLIMITED COMPANIES

Technically, it is possible to incorporate a company which does not enjoy a limited status (2006 Act, s 9(2)(c)). Therefore, if an unlimited company cannot meet its debts, its members having unlimited liability may personally have to settle the debt; consequently, all of their assets (up to the value of the debt) are at risk, so this type of company is very rare. However, it does enjoy the privilege of financial confidentiality, in that it does not have to submit accounts to the Registrar so can be used, *inter alia*, within a group of companies to keep particular assets from being disclosed to the public or at arm's length.

PRIVATE COMPANIES LIMITED BY SHARES

Legislation

Limited liability companies are primarily governed by the 2006 Act and common law, although it should be noted that the Companies Act 1985 ("1985 Act"), has not been entirely repealed and some provisions remain in force. The 2006 Act received Royal Assent on 8 November 2006 and it represents the most extensive review of company law in the last two decades.

Legal personality

A private company limited by shares cannot exist without the appointment of officers and the existence of shareholders. Despite this fact, a company is a separate legal entity distinct from its members. In reality this means that a company can enter into contracts, hold property in its own name, sue and be sued. This principle was first referred to in the case of *Salomon* v *A Salomon & Co Ltd* (1897) and is known as the "veil of incorporation". In 1892, Mr Salomon decided to incorporate a company limited by shares and Mr Salomon, his wife, daughter and four sons subscribed for one share each in the company. Following incorporation, Mr Salomon sold his boot-making business to the company for a high but not fraudulent price. The new company, having very little share capital, was unable to pay for the boot-making business entirely in cash, so the debt was settled as follows:

- issue of 20,000 shares to Mr Salomon (no other shares beyond the 20,007 were issued by the company);
- issue of a debenture, secured by a floating charge against the company's assets; and
- outstanding value in cash

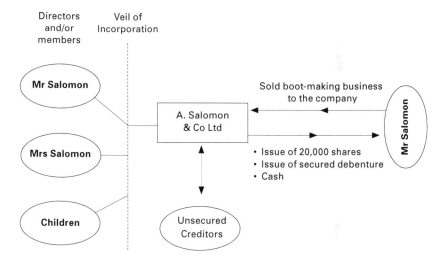

Mr Salomon's company got into financial trouble and a liquidator was appointed. It ultimately transpired that if Mr Salomon's secured debenture was valid, and therefore settled by the company, all the unsecured creditors (eg trade creditors) would receive nothing. The unsecured creditors raised an action on the basis that the debenture was not valid. The House of Lords held that the company "was not the mere 'alias' or agent of or trustee for [Mr Salomon]". Consequently, Mr Salomon was not personally required to indemnify the company's unsecured creditors (it was noted in the case that there was no fraud involved in respect of the company's creditors).

The court held that an incorporated company is a distinct legal person (all requirements of the Companies Act 1862 were complied with), therefore, A Salomon & Co Ltd could legally contract with Mr Salomon for the purchase of his boot-making business. Consequently, Mr Salomon was entitled to the last of the company's assets in satisfaction of his secured debenture.

Furthermore, when a third party contracts with a limited company there is always an inherent risk that the company may be unable to meet its debts. The veil of incorporation generally protects the members of the company from liability (discussed below are examples where the veil of incorporation has been lifted). In the case of Salomon the creditors knew they were contracting with a limited company and not Mr Salomon and accordingly he could not be held personally liable. In the case of *Lee* v *Lee's Air Farming Ltd* (1960), the fact that the company enjoyed a separate legal personality meant it could contract with its own director/shareholder. Lee's Air Farming Ltd ("the Company") was incorporated in 1954 to carry on the business of aerial top-dressing. Geoffrey Woodhouse Lee ("Lee") was the majority shareholder and a director in the Company. The Company's articles included the following:

> "33. The company shall employ the said Geoffrey Woodhouse Lee as the chief pilot of the company at a salary of £1,500 per annum from the date of incorporation of the company and in respect of such employment the rules of law applicable to the relationship of master and servant shall apply as between the company and the said Geoffrey Woodhouse Lee."

Following the correct procedures, Lee was duly employed by the Company. In 1956, while working for the Company, his aircraft crashed and he died. In order for Lee's wife to claim compensation in respect of his death under the Workers' Compensation Act 1922, of New Zealand ("1922 Act") Mrs Lee was required to satisfy, *inter alia*, s 3(1) of the 1922 Act, which stated; that where "personal injury by accident arising out of and in the course of the employment is caused to a worker, his employer shall be liable to pay compensation". A "worker" in terms of the legislation was; "any person who has entered into or works under a contract of service ... with an employer ... whether remunerated by wages, salary, or otherwise" (1922 Act, s 2).

The fundamental question was whether an employment relationship could exist between Lee and the Company? The New Zealand government was unsuccessful in its argument that it could not because Lee was the majority shareholder (3,000 shares in issue and Lee held 2,999 shares) and director of the Company. The court held that Lee and the Company were separate legal entities and therefore a valid contract of services could be entered into. As such, Lee was deemed a "worker" in terms of the legislation and Mrs Lee was consequently entitled to compensation for his death.

A company enjoying a separate legal personality is not always beneficial, as is demonstrated in the case of *Macaura* v *Northern Assurance Co Ltd* (1925). In December 1919, Mr Macaura (who owned a timber estate) sold all the timber on his estate to the company Irish Canadian Sawmills Ltd ("the Company"), in return for the allotment of 42,000 fully paid-up shares (Mr Macaura was also an unsecured creditor of the Company). Thereafter, Mr Macaura took out insurance policies in respect of the timber and executed the policies in his own name. The timber was subsequently destroyed in a fire and, despite Mr Macaura owning a significant proportion of the shares in the company, and being their largest creditor, the insurance company successfully argued that Mr Macaura had no insurable interest in the timber and therefore it did not have to settle the claim. The timber should have been insured in the name of the Company.

Ordinarily the "veil of incorporation" protects members and directors of a company from liability; however, there are certain circumstances where the "veil" may be lifted under statute or common law.

Lifting the veil under statute

Primarily, the legislation involved in lifting the veil of incorporation would be the 2006 Act, the Insolvency Act 1986 ("1986 Act") and the Company Directors Disqualification Act 1986 ("CDDA 1986"). For example, the following situations would result in the veil being lifted:

- a company has gone into insolvent liquidation and its directors thereafter become involved with another company with a similar name (1986 Act, s 216);
- a director is disqualified under the CDDA 1986, but nonetheless takes up a directorship; or
- members of a company are denied their pre-emption rights (2006 Act, s 563(2)).

Lifting the veil under common law

Common law also provides guidance on circumstances where the veil of incorporation, may be lifted, as was seen in the case of *Gilford Motor Co Ltd* v *Horne* (1933). Edward Bert Horne ("Horne") was appointed managing director of Gilford Motor Co Ltd ("Gilford"), in September 1928. Clause 9 of the contract stated:

> "The managing director shall not at any time while he shall hold the office of a managing director or afterwards solicit, interfere with or endeavour to entice away from the company any person, firm or company who at any time during or at the date of the determination of the employment of the managing director were customers of or in the habit of dealing with the company."

Following Horne's dismissal by Gilford, he set up a company named J M Horne & Co Ltd ("the Company") with his wife. The Company was essentially in competition with Gilford and consequently Gilford was successful in obtaining an injunction against both Horne and the Company. Horne appealed the decision, arguing that the covenant did not apply, as he was not personally soliciting clients. The Court of Appeal rejected his argument. Lord Hanworth MR (at 956) stated:

> "I am quite satisfied that this company was formed as a device, a stratagem, in order to mask the effective carrying on of a business of Mr. E. B. Horne. The purpose of it was to try to enable him, under what is a cloak or a sham, to engage in business ..."

The courts recognised that the Company was a separate legal entity but that it had been created in order for Horne to evade the contract concluded with Gilford. Abusing a corporate vehicle is not acceptable and where such a sham or facade occurs the courts will look beyond the veil of incorporation.

What about where companies are closely linked in a group – can the veil of incorporation be lifted to enable the group to be treated as one entity? This issue was considered in *DHN Food Distributors Ltd* v *Tower Hamlets London Borough Council* (1976). A group of three companies were involved in the distribution of food. DHN Food Distributors Ltd ("DHN") was the parent company and it owned the business. The two wholly owned subsidiary companies played different roles within the business. Bronze Investments Ltd ("Bronze") owned the business premises and DHN Food Transport Ltd ("Transport") owned and managed the business's vehicles. The directors in both subsidiary companies were the same as in DHN.

Tower Hamlets London Borough Council issued a compulsory purchase order in respect of the business premises owned by Bronze. The three companies endeavoured to find suitable alternative premises in which to operate their business but with no success and subsequently DHN, Bronze and Transport all went into liquidation.

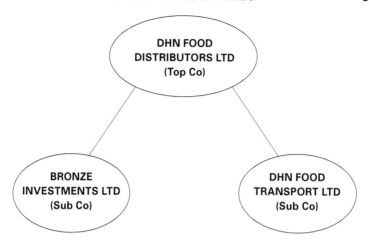

One of the issues considered in this case was whether DHN and Transport were entitled to compensation. Compensation was payable under two heads: (i) the value of the land; and (ii) disturbance of the business (under the Land Compensation Act 1961, s 5(2) and (6)). To be successful under both heads, a company technically needed to both own and occupy the premises and this was not the case. Arguably the most straightforward approach would have been to transfer the premises (owned by Bronze) to DHN (with no stamp duty liability), thus satisfying the owner-occupier criteria for compensation. This would have been possible as Bronze was entirely controlled by DHN. This was not done.

The Court of Appeal (Lord Denning) held that the veil of incorporation should be lifted and that all three companies should be entitled to compensation. This case established the "Group Entity Theory", thereby allowing companies that are closely linked to each other to be treated as one. Although the case of *DHN* has not been specifically overruled, subsequent cases have distinguished it, including the Scottish case of *Woolfson* v *Strathclyde Regional Council* (1978). Several shop units in Glasgow's St George's Road were owned by Mr Solomon Woolfson ("Woolfson") and Solfred Holdings Ltd ("Solfred"). The units were occupied by M & L Campbell (Glasgow) Ltd ("Campbell"), which carried on a business specialising in wedding gowns. The shareholders in Solfred and Campbell were Woolfson and his wife. As in the case of *DHN Food Distributors Ltd* (discussed above), Strathclyde Regional Council issued a compulsory purchase order for the premises in St George's Road. Again,

OWNERS OF THE PREMISES

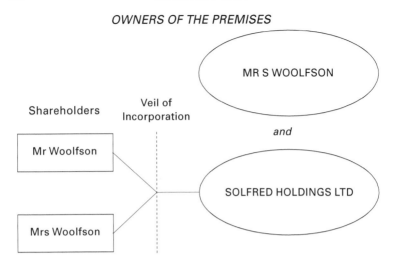

OCCUPIERS OF THE PREMISES

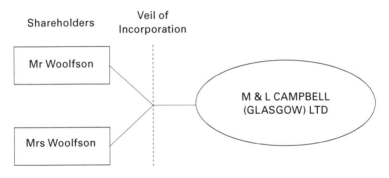

in order to qualify for full compensation the owner and occupier of the premises had to be the same person.

Woolfson and Solfred, as owners of the units, sought compensation for loss of their premises and for disturbance to the business. They argued that in reality the business being carried on by Campbell was theirs and that Campbell was simply their agent. Consequently, they were entitled to full compensation (relying on *DHN*); and Woolfson, Solfred and Campbell should not be viewed as separate legal entities, rather they should be grouped together as one.

It was held that the distinct legal persona enjoyed by an incorporated company, as established by *Salomon*, cannot simply be overlooked. The court held that Campbell was not a "mere shell or facade but a company *de facto* engaged in business" and the veil of incorporation should only be lifted in exceptional circumstances. Furthermore, the court held that the facts of the case were sufficiently different to *DHN* and could be distinguished on that basis. It should be noted that the decision in Woolfson has subsequently been referred to with approval (*Adams* v *Cape Industries plc* (1990)). Furthermore, in the case of *Ord* v *Belhaven Pubs Ltd* (1998) the court held that where an individual contracts with a company and subsequently brings an action against them, they cannot seek to substitute the defender with an associated company, by piercing the veil, particularly where there is no suggestion of impropriety. Essentially, you cannot pierce the veil of incorporation simply to provide justice for the pursuer.

Result of lifting the veil

Where the "veil" is lifted, the limited liability which members and directors ordinarily enjoy is removed and they may become personally liable for their acts and/or omissions. Usually this will result in a personal contribution to the company's assets, although in some circumstances the bringing of a criminal prosecution is possible.

Essential Facts

- There are various different types of companies, including: public limited companies; companies limited by guarantee; unlimited companies; and private companies limited by shares.
- There are several significant differences between public limited companies ("plc") and private companies limited by shares, including the requirement for a plc to have a trading certificate (2006 Act, s 761) and the requirement to have a minimum of two directors (2006 Act, s 154(2)).
- Once incorporated, a company is a separate legal entity distinct from its directors and members.
- The veil of incorporation that protects members and directors from personal liability can be lifted both under common law and statute.

Essential Cases

Salomon v A Salomon Co Ltd (1897): refers to the principle known as the "veil of incorporation", which protects members of a company from liability. It is accepted that in certain circumstances the "veil" may be lifted and directors/members may become personally liable for their acts and/or omissions.

Lee v Lee's Air Farming Ltd (1960): considers the principle that a company is a separate legal entity distinct from its officers and members. It was held in this case that being a director and shareholder in a company did not preclude a person from entering into a valid employment contract with the company.

Macaura v Northern Assurance Co Ltd (1925): demonstrates that a company being viewed as a distinct legal entity is not always beneficial. This case resulted in an insurance company successfully refusing to pay out under a policy, as it was executed in the name of the company's shareholder rather than in the name of the company.

Gilford Motor Co Ltd v Horne (1933): considers a situation where the veil of incorporation is lifted. The court held that the company was being used as a means to avoid a prior contractual obligation and in essence there was an abuse of the corporate vehicle.

DHN Food Distributors Ltd v Tower Hamlets London Borough Council (1976): refers to the "group entity" theory. Where a group of companies were so closely linked that the veil of incorporation was lifted, they were treated as a single entity. This case has not been overruled, but has notably been disparaged.

Woolfson v Strathclyde Regional Council (1978): distinguishes itself from the case of *DHN Food Distributors Ltd*. This case concluded that a company has a separate legal personality and this cannot be overlooked, unless exceptional circumstances exist.

5 PRE-INCORPORATION

There is no statutory definition provided as to who is a "promoter". It is generally determined as a matter of fact after considering the actions of a person. However, it is important to note that a professional person (for example a solicitor or an accountant) providing services in the setting up of a company will not be deemed a promoter of the company.

Before a company is incorporated, it has no legal status and therefore no capacity to enter into contracts. However, it is sometimes necessary, in anticipation of a company's incorporation, for transactions to be concluded and property purchased. This is often done by a promoter, who will usually become one of the first directors of the company. A promoter's relationship with a company cannot be described as one of agency, given that a company, pre-incorporation, is not a distinct legal entity. The relationship is fiduciary in nature, and, as such, promoters owe certain duties to a company including a duty to disclose any benefits they personally receive in connection with its promotion.

Where there is a breach of duty by a promoter, remedies include:

- rescission of the contract (although it is important to note that this option is not always available, eg where the parties cannot be returned to their pre-contractual position or third party rights have intervened);
- seeking damages (*Re Leeds and Hanley Theatres of Varieties Ltd* (1904));
- suing for return of profit made (*Gluckstein* v *Barnes* (1900)); or
- bringing derivative proceedings under ss 265-269 of the Companies Act 2006 ("2006 Act") (see Chapter 11).

PRE-INCORPORATION CONTRACT

Sometimes a promoter will enter into a contract for the benefit of a company prior to incorporation (eg to obtain premises or equipment). In entering such an agreement there are intrinsic risks that promoters should be aware of. The position at common law has not been entirely clear.

Development of common law

In *Tinnevelly Sugar Refining Co Ltd* v *Mirrlees, Watson and Yaryan Co Ltd* (1894), prior to the incorporation of Tinnevelly its promoters entered into a contract for the supply of machinery from the defenders. When Tinnevelly was incorporated it received the machinery, but it was defective. The court held that Tinnevelly had no title to sue in respect of a pre-incorporation contract.

In *Kelner* v *Baxter* (1866), a promoter acting for a pre-incorporated company was held personally liable in relation to the agreement entered into with the third party. It is not possible for a company to ratify the actions of a promoter (once incorporated) as it was not in existence at the time of execution of the contract.

The case of *Kelner* did not create a clear rule on the issue and distinctions have been made subsequently. In *Newborne* v *Sensolid (Great Britain) Ltd* (1954), an agreement purported to be entered into between a pre-incorporated company and a third party was held as not to constitute a legally binding contract. Arguably, the courts will consider the manner and intention of the parties at the time of execution of the agreement.

Companies Act 2006, s 51

Legislation has brought some much needed clarity in relation to liability under a contract entered into by a promoter on behalf of a pre-incorporated company:

> "A contract that purports to be made by or on behalf of a company at a time when the company has not been formed has effect, subject to any agreement to the contrary, as one made with the person purporting to act for the company or as agent for it, and he is personally liable on the contract accordingly" (2006 Act, s 51(1)).

Section 51 of the 2006 Act applies only where incorporation of a company is anticipated, but has not yet come to fruition, yet a promoter nonetheless feels obliged to enter into a contract on its behalf. In these circumstances, it is possible that a third party may agree not to hold the promoter personally liable. While technically feasible under the 2006 Act, it remains unlikely that a third party would enter into a contract and relinquish any right of recourse against the other contracting party. Arguably, there would be little point in executing the contract: the third party would be afforded greater protection by waiting for the company to be incorporated.

The case of *Phonogram Ltd* v *Lane* (1981), considered the effect of what is now s 51 of the 2006 Act. A contract was purported to be entered into between Phonogram Ltd and "Fragile Management Ltd" (a pre-incorporated company) and was signed "for and on behalf" of the unformed company by Brian Lane ("the Promoter"). Following execution of the contract, Phonogram Ltd advanced financial support in order to help start the business. However, no company was ever incorporated and Phonogram Ltd sought recovery of their money (£6,000) from the Promoter.

The Promoter was held personally liable to repay the money advanced as he was purporting to act on behalf of a company prior to incorporation. "A contact can purport to be made on behalf of a company ... even though that company is known by both parties not to be formed ..." (Lord Denning MR at 943). Given that now there is a greater degree of clarity on the matter, the decision in Newborne in all likelihood would be reversed.

Avoiding promoter's liability

It has been established that a promoter, while acting on a pre-incorporated company's behalf, is personally liable in relation to all contracts entered into, unless express agreement is made to the contrary with a third party (2006 Act, s 51). This means that, where a third party relinquishes a promoter from personal liability, they would be unable to sue the promoter if the company did not subsequently comply with the terms of the contract.

However, given the promoter's potential exposure to personal liability in respect of pre-incorporation transactions, a number of options are available to them in order to mitigate this risk, including the following:

- the purchase of an off-the-shelf company. This type of company is generally available from most commercial law firms. It is an incorporated company that can be tailored to your needs very quickly, eg appointment of new directors/shareholders. It can then be used to enter into contracts.

    Alternatively, wait until incorporation of a company – it is possible to organise same-day incorporation, provided it is received by the Registrar before 3pm (see Companies House for details);

- the promoter and third party agree on a draft contract to be executed by the company on incorporation. This protects the promoter from liability as he never enters into a contract. However, it may be unsatisfactory for the third party as there is no legal obligation on the company to sign the contract and therefore the third party has no protection or legal redress; or

- 2006 Act, s 51 provides that a promoter will not be personally liable if an "agreement to the contrary" is entered into with the third party (discussed above).

Where a promoter does enter into a contract on behalf of a pre-incorporated company, the company may relieve the promoter from liability if the contract is novated.

Essential Facts

- There is no statutory definition of who is a "promoter".
- While the relationship between a promoter and a pre-incorporated company cannot be described as one of agency, it is fiduciary in nature, and as such a promoter owes a number of duties.
- There was little consistency at common law regarding liability when a promoter entered into a contract on behalf of a pre-incorporated company with a third party. Section 51 of the 2006 Act provides clarity on the situation.
- Pursuant to s 51 of the 2006 Act, a promoter will be personally liable under a contract entered into on behalf of a pre-incorporated company, unless there is agreement to the contrary. Promoters should be aware of this risk and seek to mitigate it.

Essential Case

Phonogram Ltd v Lane (1981): this case considers the effect of what is now s 51 of the 2006 Act. The promoter of a company will be held personally liable in relation to a contract purported to be made on behalf of a company.

6 INCORPORATION OF A PRIVATE COMPANY LIMITED BY SHARES

To incorporate a company, a Form IN01 (see Companies House) must be delivered to the Registrar of Companies together with a Memorandum of Association ("Memorandum"), Articles of Association ("Articles") and an incorporation fee, pursuant to s 9 of the Companies Act 2006 (the "2006 Act"). If a set of Articles is not delivered, the Registrar will assume that the company is adopting the model Articles without alteration (2006 Act, s 20). Provided that the documents are accepted by the Registrar, a certificate of incorporation will be issued. It is at this point that a company is seen as a separate legal entity and can contract in its own name. The content and purpose of each incorporation document will be considered in turn.

INCORPORATION DOCUMENTS

Form IN01

- Company name – a number of restrictions and requirements need to be considered when selecting a company name. The end of the name must include the word "Limited" or "Ltd" (2006 Act, s 59), there cannot be a company with the same or similar name already incorporated, and certain restrictions apply in relation to the use of particular words (2006 Act, ss 53–56 and under common law).
- Registered office – a company's official address. It is available to view at Companies House and will appear on all official documentation of a company (eg its annual return). A company is legally required always to have a registered office in order that communications and notices may be directly received by it. It also indicates where the company books are held (2006 Act, s 114), which is important since the register of members is open to inspection by a company's members and/or third parties (2006 Act, s 116).
- Directors – the officers of a company. It is possible for a company to be incorporated with one director (2006 Act, s 154(1)), and there is no upper statutory limit on the number of directors, provided no restrictions exist in a company's Articles. While it remains possible to have "corporate directors", under the 2006 Act all companies must have a minimum of one human director.

- It is now possible under the 2006 Act for directors to provide a "service address", which is usually the same as the company's registered office, rather than providing their own residential address for public consumption.

- Company secretary – an officer of a company with ostensible authority to contract on a company's behalf (*Panorama Developments (Guildford) Ltd* v *Fidelis Furnishing Fabrics Ltd* (1971)). Under s 270 of the 2006 Act there is now no requirement for a private company to have a company secretary although they may continue to do so if they wish (see Chapter 18).

- Subscribers – the first shareholders of a company. They, or an agent on behalf of them, must sign and date the IN01 Form. This form provides a statement of the proposed capital of a company, together with details of their individual shareholding.

    Section 9(1) of the 2006 Act provides that a statutory declaration be completed which should be signed by all subscribers (or an agent on their behalf) verifying that all the requirements pertaining to the incorporation of a company have been complied with (2006 Act, s 13(1)).

Memorandum of Association

The Memorandum under the 2006 Act has a decidedly different format and a more limited purpose. However, this does not negate its importance. The Memorandum requires each subscriber to sign it, and it will detail the number of shares being issued to them (2006 Act, s 8(1)(b)). The most significant changes under the 2006 Act are that the Memorandum can no longer be amended once a company has been incorporated and it no longer contains an objects clause.

Articles of Association

Articles primarily govern the relationship between members of a company, and there are no statutory requirements relating to the type of information which should be included in a company's Articles. Typical Articles will include details on the appointment and removal of officers of a company, and the process of convening meetings. It is not uncommon for companies simply to adopt the model Articles (SI 2008/3229), in whole or in part. It remains possible, following incorporation, for a company's Articles to be altered, provided that they do not attempt to circumvent the applicability of legislation.

Ordinarily, a company's Articles can be amended by the passing of a special resolution; however, under the 2006 Act it is now possible for provisions within a company's Articles to be entrenched (2006 Act, s 22). Where an article has been entrenched it cannot be amended or removed unless particular conditions are met or procedures are adhered to (2006 Act, s 22(1)). It is possible to entrench an article at the point of incorporation, or when the company is formed by unanimous consent of all the shareholders (2006 Act, s 22(2)). The Registrar of Companies must be notified if any entrenched articles are amended or removed (2006 Act, s 23).

MEMBERSHIP CONTRACT

"The provisions of a company's constitution bind the company and its members to the same extent as if there were covenants on the part of the company and of each member to observe those provisions" (2006 Act, s 33(1)).

The Articles (and Memorandum) of a company provide a contract governing the relationship between the company and its members (*Beattie v E&F Beattie Ltd* (1938)). They are subject to the 2006 Act so cannot be drafted in order to circumvent provisions within the legislation, or be amended by the court. Articles can be altered by special resolution (2006 Act, s 21(1)), which means the contract between the company and shareholders may also be subject to amendment (*Brown v British Abrasive Wheel Co Ltd* (1919)). Given that the contract is between the company and its members, no other party may prevent a company from amending its Articles (*Southern Foundries (1926) Ltd v Shirlaw* (1940)). Articles may only be amended if it is *bona fide* in the interests of the entire company.

CONSIDERATIONS BEFORE INCORPORATION

When contemplating incorporating a private company limited by shares it is important to consider whether this type of limited company is the most appropriate business vehicle to meet your needs. While this is certainly not an exhaustive list, some advantages and disadvantages include the following.

Advantages

- A company has a separate legal personality and can enter into contracts, hold property in its own name, sue and be sued.

- Perpetual succession – there is no transfer of assets when a member joins or leaves a company.
- Members have, in most circumstances, limited liability.
- Can assist in raising finance.
- There is no maximum statutory limit to the number of members in a company (limits may be laid down in its Articles).
- The 2006 Act (remaining parts of the 1985 Act), common law and a company's constitutional documents provide a readily available source of guidance.

Disadvantages

- Certain expenses will be incurred in incorporating a company.
- There are certain limitations on the name a company can choose.
- Increased formality, which includes the passing of resolutions and completing annual returns and accounts.
- A company is required to file certain information with the Registrar of Companies, thus putting information in the public domain.
- Limited liability in certain circumstances may be illusory: for example, directors may be required to provide personal guarantees.

Essential Facts

- Incorporation is primarily governed by the Companies Act 2006.
- Section 9 of the 2006 Act stipulates the information that must be delivered to the Registrar of Companies in order to incorporate a company.
- A company, once incorporated, is seen as a separate legal entity.
- Members enjoy limited liability provided the "veil of incorporation" is not lifted.
- A company's constitution provides a contract that governs the relationship between a company and its members (2006 Act, s 33).

7 MEETINGS AND RESOLUTIONS

Meetings of company members can be categorised as either general or class meetings, and are called in order to deal with the business of a company. The law regulating both categories of meeting is largely the same, pursuant to ss 301–333 of the Companies Act 2006 ("2006 Act"), although a number of exceptions are detailed in s 334 of the 2006 Act.

CATEGORIES OF MEETINGS

Annual General Meeting ("AGM")

A private limited company is now no longer under an obligation to hold an AGM; however, it can opt to do so. Often the primary reasons for holding an AGM are to allow a company's accounts to be laid before its members, for the members to appoint auditors and for the payment of dividends to be approved. Under the 2006 Act, there remains an obligation for public limited companies ("plcs") to continue to convene AGMs. An AGM must be held within 6 months from the company's individual accounting reference date. (2006 Act, s 336(1)). In order for a plc to convene an AGM, 21 days' notice (2006 Act, s 307(2)) must be given, in writing (2006 Act, s 337(1)), to company members, although it is possible to convene an AGM on short notice, provided that there is unanimous consent by all members (2006 Act, s 337(2)).

General Meeting ("GM")

A GM is usually convened by the directors of a company when requisitioned by members who hold at least 5 per cent of the paid-up share capital of a company (2006 Act, s 303). The directors shall within 21 days from receipt of a requisition proceed to convene a GM and this should be held within 28 days from the date of the notice convening the meeting (2006 Act, s 304).

Notice of a GM must be given to all the members, in writing, 14 days before the GM (2006 Act, s 307(1)). Notice may be provided in a number of forms including hardcopy, electronic form, or by website (2006 Act, s 308). It is possible for a company's Articles of Association ("Articles") to stipulate a longer notice period (2006 Act, s 307(3)). It is also possible for a GM to be called on short notice, provided that at least 90 per cent of the members concur (2006 Act, s 307(6)).

Class meetings

This type of meeting is held by a particular class of shareholders, where decisions affecting only that class of shares are being taken: for example, varying their class rights. The notice must clearly state the location, time, general nature of the business, and type of general meeting being convened. Notice must be validly served on every member.

Board meetings

Generally, directors of larger companies will convene monthly board meetings to deal with business matters. The Articles of Association (SI 2008/3229) ("Model Articles") do provide some guidance, although directors are free to adopt their own rules to govern these meetings. Ordinarily, minutes of board meetings are recorded, which sometimes proves useful as *prima facie* evidence of their decision-making process should they be pursued, *inter alia*, for a breach of their directors' duties. While this represents good practice, unfortunately it does not always occur, particularly in single-member companies and family-run companies. However, it remains prudent to have them should auditors, solicitors, liquidators or the courts subsequently have to examine a decision.

PROCEDURE OF MEETINGS

Quorum

No business can be dealt with in a general meeting (other than appointing a chairman) if it is not quorate. The 2006 Act states that in a single member limited company the quorum is set at one "qualifying person", and in all other cases is two (2006 Act, s 318). However, the Articles should always be consulted as this number may be varied.

Proxies

When a shareholder is unable to attend a meeting they have a statutory right to appoint a proxy to attend and vote in their absence (2006 Act, s 324(1)). All notices issued in order to convene a meeting must state that members enjoy this right. Failure to do so does not invalidate the meeting; however, officers of the company are liable to criminal conviction (2006 Act, s 325). The right to appoint a proxy extends to every share held by a shareholder, so it is possible to appoint multiple proxies, provided they are exercising rights which are attached to different shares (2006 Act, s 324(2)). Furthermore, a company's Articles should always be consulted as they may require specific details to be included in the proxy notice or stipulate the method of its delivery (Model Article 45).

Voting

Generally, a shareholders' vote is exercised by a show of hands in a general meeting (ie one shareholder equals one vote) (Model Article 42). However, if requested, a vote can be taken by way of a poll provided it is carried out in line with the company's Articles (Model Article 44). This means that a member's voting rights are proportionate to the number of shares they hold (2006 Act, s 284(3)).

RESOLUTIONS

A resolution records a decision made by the members (or particular class of members) of a company. There are different resolutions which may be passed by members in general meetings; and in certain circumstances the 2006 Act specifies the type of resolution to be passed.

Type of resolution	Voting requirements
Ordinary	Simple majority
Special	75% or more

As an alternative to passing one of the above resolutions in a general meeting, the 2006 Act provides that a written resolution may be passed in its place. A written resolution requires the same level of consent from company's members entitled to vote on a specific matter, as would be required in a general meeting. For a written resolution to be effective, the requisite percentage of members must sign the resolution (2006 Act, s 296).

The undernoted table provides a number of examples of the type of resolution to be passed in particular circumstances:

Issue	Type of resolution	2006 Act
Change of company name	Special	s 78(1)
Alteration of Articles	Special	s 21
Removal of a director	Ordinary	s 168

The Articles of a company may provide additional requirements and/or restrictions and should be consulted before any resolution is proposed.

Duomatic principle

In the case of *Re Duomatic Ltd* (1969), over a period of years directors withdrew remuneration (based on their individual needs) without first obtaining shareholder approval, as was required. It was held that, given that all the shareholders had consented to this action, despite no formal resolution having been passed, the circumstances would nonetheless be treated as if the necessary resolution had been duly passed at a general meeting.

Essential Facts

- Members can hold either general meetings or class meetings (plcs must hold Annual General Meetings and private limited companies may elect to do so).
- The notice period of meetings depends on the type of meeting and the nature of business intended to be dealt with.
- Resolutions are decisions taken by members of a company.

8 DIRECTORS

Directors can be described as officers of a company. The term "director", when used in terms of the Companies Act 2006 ("2006 Act"), is taken to include any persons "occupying the position of director, by whatever named called" (2006 Act, s 250). However, it is important to note, while a director must have a legal persona, at least one of the directors must be a *natural person* (2006 Act, s 155).

The number of directors a company is able to appoint is often dictated by the Articles of Association (SI 2008/3229) ("Model Articles"), together with details on the method of appointment (Model Article 17). However, despite the requirement to adhere to the Articles of Association ("Articles"), if any defect exists in relation to a director's appointment this will not adversely affect the validity of any of his acts (2006 Act, s 161). In terms of the 2006 Act, there are no formal qualifications required to become a director; however, a company's Articles may provide certain stipulations or restrictions and certain individuals can be disqualified under the Company Directors Disqualification Act 1986 (discussed below).

Directors are under a duty to comply both with the provisions of a company's constitutional documents and with current legislation. The obligations can on occasion be onerous, and may include how a director should manage the company, take major decisions or enter into substantial contracts. A director's main responsibility is to manage the company and this will predominately focus on commercial and administrative matters. Shareholders are often very happy with this arrangement as they may not have the necessary expertise or indeed inclination to run a company. They are often simply content to receive a sufficient dividend by way of return on their investment.

TYPES OF DIRECTORS

Given the responsibilities placed on directors, it is perhaps unhelpful that who constitutes a director is not clearly defined. Consequently, there are various recognised types of directors, and they include the following:

- de facto *director* – not formally appointed to the board but professes to act as a director of a company;

- *shadow director* – an individual who has not been formally appointed as a director but who, as a matter of fact, influences the decisions of a company;
- *alternate director* – appointed by an existing director to perform all the functions of the appointer in their absence;
- *nominee director* – members have a specific right to appoint, remove and/or replace one or more of these directors, eg in joint venture companies;
- *executive director* – an individual who is ordinarily an employee of the company and undertakes an executive role; or
- *non-executive director* – an individual who typically would hold a directorship and is appointed primarily due to their skills, knowledge or connections.

DIRECTORS' DUTIES

The relationship between a director and a company can be described as fiduciary in nature. Historically, a number of fiduciary duties under common law were owed by a director to a company and they included the following:

- to act for the benefit of a company as a whole and not to fetter their discretion;
- to avoid conflicts between their personal interests and the interests of a company; and
- to act honestly and in good faith when making decisions affecting a company.

A director also owed a duty of care, skill and diligence to a company. This was measured objectively, with a comparison being made to another person holding a similar directorship, and subjectively to the extent that consideration is given to what can be reasonably expected from a director with their level of experience, skill and knowledge.

Codification of duties under the 2006 Act

Directors' duties established at common law have now been put into a statutory framework under the 2006 Act. However, the underlying principles have, on the whole, remained unchanged. It is the intention that these new statutory duties will be interpreted and applied in the same way as they were under common law.

Pursuant to s 170 of the 2006 Act, directors owe general duties to their respective companies and these duties are detailed in ss 171–177 of the 2006 Act.

Duty to act within powers (2006 Act, s 171)

This duty simply codifies the previous common law position, that directors should act within their powers and exercise their powers for proper purpose. Previously directors would have been required to consult their company's Memorandum of Association ("the Memorandum") and Articles. However, under the 2006 Act the Memorandum now contains very limited information, so the Articles would be the primary document for directors to consult.

Duty to promote the success of the company (2006 Act, s 172)

In codifying current law, the 2006 Act introduces a new duty on a director to "act in the way he considers, in good faith, would be most likely to promote the success of the company for the benefit of its members as a whole" (2006 Act, s 172). This replaces the previous duty to act "in good faith and in the best interests of the company". This new duty of promoting a company's success highlights a major shift in the way companies will have to undertake their business. This new duty requires companies, *inter alia*, to consider six broad social factors (2006 Act, s 172(1)):

- the likely long-term consequences of any decision;
- the interests of the company's employees;
- fostering business relationships, including those of customer and supplier;
- the effect of the company's operations on the community and the environment;
- the desirability of the company maintaining a reputation for high standards of business conduct; and
- the need to act fairly as between members of the company.

This duty represents an all-encompassing fiduciary duty owed by directors to their companies and provides not an insignificant list of factors which directors must consider when making a business decision. It is not inconceivable that a director may make a decision which ultimately is in the best interests of the company but does not meet one or more of these social factors. Does this automatically mean that a director has breached their duty to the company? When considering a director's decision, a subjective approach must be taken. A director will not be in breach of discharging this duty provided they can demonstrate that they considered these social factors and on balance considered other factors to be of more importance to the company in that particular situation. In all likelihood this would be considered an acceptable discharge of director's duties (it would be important to make sure that a proper record of the decision-making process was made).

This new duty provides a significant change in the way a company must consider its business ventures. Previously, companies often focused on the short-term consequences of their business decisions but now they are required to consider the long-term impact (2006 Act, s 172(1)(a)).

Duty to exercise independent judgement (2006 Act, s 173)

Prior to the implementation of the 2006 Act there were fairly strict rules governing directors. It was the intention of the 2006 Act to lessen these restrictions which prevent a director from having an interest that may potentially conflict with the company's interests. Despite this objective, some may argue that, following the codification of this duty, the rules are now more burdensome. Undoubtedly, this may deter directors from taking multiple directorships or individuals from taking non-executive directorships. Arguably, only time will tell if there is such a negative impact.

This duty requires directors to approach company matters without bias. This open-minded approach places a duty on directors to exercise judgement and that it be done independently. Where a director has legally bound themself in the future to take a particular course of action, arguably they are in breach of this duty. However, there are two exceptions to the general rule (2006 Act, s 173(2)), provided they have acted *bona fide* in the best interests of the company:

- where a contractual agreement has been entered into on behalf of the company which restricts its future exercise of discretionary powers, there is no breach even though this has fettered their discretion; and
- if a company's Articles allow a director to restrict the exercise of their independent judgement.

Duty to exercise reasonable care, skill and diligence (2006 Act, s 174)

This is the only non-fiduciary duty and it has simplified the common law duty of care and skill. The legislation provides guidance on the degree of "care, skill and diligence" that is required to be exercised by a director (2006 Act, s 174(1)).

The courts, when deciding whether this duty has been properly discharged by a director, must take both an objective and a subjective approach, pursuant to s 174(2) of the 2006 Act:

- *objective test*: considers what a reasonable person would expect from a hypothetical director, giving specific consideration to the general knowledge, skill and experience that could reasonably be expected of a director acting on behalf of a company; and
- *subjective test*: consideration must be given to the actual skill set and knowledge of a particular director – this could patently increase the standard of care expected.

In the case of *Re D'Jan of London Ltd* (1993), Mr D'Jan was a director (and majority shareholder) of a company and as such had the responsibility to make sure the company had the necessary insurance policies in place. Mr D'Jan neglected to properly check the insurance documentation of the company, which contained inaccuracies. Following a devastating fire which engulfed the company premises and destroyed its stock, the insurance company was able to repudiate the contract on the basis of these inaccuracies.

The company ultimately became insolvent and the liquidator (on behalf of its unsecured creditors) successfully pursued proceedings against Mr D'Jan on the basis that he had breached his "duty of care, skill and diligence". The High Court, when considering both the objective and subjective test, held that Mr D'Jan was negligent in his discharge of this duty. Consequently, Mr D'Jan was liable to compensate the company. However, pursuant to s 727 of the Companies Act 1985 (now 2006 Act, s 1157), a director may be relieved either wholly or partially of their liability if the court believes that they have "acted honestly and reasonably [in the circumstances and] ought fairly to be excused". Mr D'Jan was awarded partial relief from his liabilities, as the court exercised this discretionary power.

Duty to avoid conflicts of interest (2006 Act, s 175)

This director's duty previously existed under the Companies Act 1985 ("1985 Act") and the 2006 Act has both amended and restated this duty. The key objective was to simplify the duty in order to facilitate transactions between directors and third parties in the business arena. However, some may argue codification has had the converse effect, and this duty is now more restrictive and may ultimately discourage directors from accepting multiple directorships.

It is important to note that this duty may be breached by a director even if the company itself could not have benefited from the information and ultimately from the transaction (ie this is not a successful defence for the director), as is demonstrated in the case of *Industrial Development Consultants* v *Cooley* (1972). Neville Cooley ("Cooley") an architect, was appointed as a managing director of Industrial Development Consultants Ltd ("IDC"), which provided construction services. The purpose of his appointment was to help IDC secure further contracts in the public sector, especially in relation to gas boards.

Cooley (on behalf of IDC) and the Eastern Gas Board ("EGB") entered into discussions about the possible construction of four depots. These negotiations were ultimately unsuccessful, as EGB made it clear that they had specific objections about the appointment of IDC.

Thereafter, EGB approached Cooley in a private capacity in connection with him designing and constructing the depots. Cooley, realising that he could personally secure this lucrative contract (likely to be in excess of £1.7m), advised IDC that he was seriously unwell and needed to be immediately released from his position within the company. Cooley then set up his own business of consultancy and project design management and obtained the contract from EGB.

On discovering this, IDC raised an action against Cooley, arguing that he must account to them for all benefits, remuneration and fees he received under the contract with EGB. The court held that Cooley, as managing director of IDC, was in a fiduciary relationship with them. Despite this, Cooley pursued a course of action that resulted in the fiduciary duty he owed to IDC being in direct conflict with his own personal interests. Cooley was under a specific obligation to pass on, for the benefit of IDC, all information he received in his capacity as managing director, and consequently should not have followed a course of action in order to personally benefit.

Ultimately, Cooley was accountable to IDC for all monies received and the fact that IDC could not ever have secured the contract itself (due to EGB's objections) was held immaterial. Although Cooley was not the managing director of IDC when he secured the contract with EGB, he had nevertheless exploited his knowledge in order to do so.

Provisions of the 2006 Act now allow for "non-conflicted directors" to approve the transaction provided that certain criteria are met (2006 Act, s 175(5) and (6)). Arguably, this makes the process easier; however, it may take some time in order to establish how this might practically benefit (or otherwise) companies.

Duty not to accept benefits from third parties (2006 Act, s 176)

This duty largely restates the position that existed at common law. Directors are prohibited from profiting from their position; this would include accepting benefits (not limited to only financial benefits) from third parties who currently deal with the company as well as those who have the potential to do so. A director will not be guilty for failing to discharge this duty if the profit received could not be perceived as presenting a conflict of interest. The reality of the situation is that it is not always evident if a benefit may be regarded as creating a conflict of interest. It remains the case that directors must be cautious in their approach to such matters.

Duty to declare interest in proposed transaction or arrangement (2006 Act, s 177)

This duty previously existed under s 317 of the 1985 Act and requires a director to declare any interest that they may have in a particular contract that the company is considering entering into. However, under the 2006 Act the requirement is now more extensive and requires a director to disclose the "nature and extent" of their interest to the board of directors. Moreover, a director is under an obligation to make a disclosure if they "ought reasonably to be aware of" the conflict and this duty extends to those "connected" to a director (2006 Act, s 252). Essentially, only in circumstances where it would be deemed; reasonable to assume no potential conflict would exist, the directors have been previously notified of the situation, or it is the director's service contract that is being considered (2006 Act, s 177(6)), would a declaration not be required.

Summary

Only time will tell if this new statutory framework provides directors with greater certainty regarding the duties they owe to their respective companies; it is undoubtedly one of the long-term goals of the 2006 Act. However, in the short-term, it will arguably be challenging for the courts to interpret and apply this new legislation in the same manner as they did before codification. Moreover, the introduction and expansion of duties could create an element of uncertainty for both directors and the courts.

Remedies for breach of directors' duties

A number of remedies will be available should a director fail to discharge their duties in terms of ss 171–177 of the 2006 Act and they are stipulated in s 178 of the 2006 Act. Consequently, where there is a breach (or potential breach) of a fiduciary duty (excludes 2006 Act, s 174), the remedies would be the same as if the "corresponding common law or equitable principle applied", and would include the following:

- compensation;
- damages;
- restoration of the company's property;
- account to the company of any profits received; or
- rescission of the contract.

While these remedies are available, a company may decide to ratify a director's act or omission which constituted the breach of the director's duties (2006 Act, ss 171–177). This is possible by the shareholders passing an ordinary resolution to that effect (2006 Act, s 239). Where ratification by the members of the company does not occur, it is still open for the courts to grant the director complete or partial relief in respect of their breach. This is only possible where the director has "acted honestly and reasonably, and that having regard to all the circumstances of the case ... ought fairly to be excused" (discussed above – 2006 Act, s 1157).

Additional statutory obligations

Beyond the codification of director's duties under the 2006 Act (ss 171–177), further statutory restrictions exist, including the following:

- Long-term service contract entered into between the company and director requires members' approval (2006 Act, ss 188–189).
- Transactions where the company buys or sells a "substantial" non-cash asset from or to a director of the company requires members' approval. Available remedies include rescission and accounting for profits received (2006 Act, ss 190–196).
- Loans or similar types of transactions by a company (or holding company) to their directors require members' consent (2006 Act, ss 197–214). Remedies again include rescission and accounting for profits received (2006 Act, s 213 exceptions to the general position are detailed in 2006 Act, ss 204–209).

- Payments by a company to a director for loss of office (2006 Act, ss 215–222).

PERSONAL LIABILITY

Directors become personally liable for their actions and/or omissions in circumstances where the "veil of incorporation" is lifted (eg 2006 Act, ss 386–389). Personal liability of directors can occur in a variety of circumstances including where a director concludes a contract (on a company's behalf) without the requisite authority, or where a director falls foul of legislative provisions. Certain sections of the Insolvency Act 1986 ("1986 Act"), if breached, may result in a director becoming personally liable, and include the following.

Fraudulent trading

It may be concluded that trading has been fraudulent under s 213 of the 1986 Act, if it appears that any business of a company has been carried out with the intent to "defraud creditors of the company or creditors of any other person, or for any fraudulent purpose" during the course of winding up a company. Where a court makes this finding, it may order that any person who knowingly was a party to this fraudulent behaviour is financially liable to contribute to a company's assets to such extent as the court deems appropriate.

Only a liquidator has the power to make an application to the court in relation to a director's fraudulent trading. By way of illustration, a liquidator may pursue an application where advanced payment for goods is accepted by a company or a company gains credit, knowing that it will not be able to repay the money on the due date (see Chapter 15).

Wrongful trading

Pursuant to s 214 of the 1986 Act, in order for a director (or shadow director) to incur personal liability, a company must have gone into insolvent liquidation and at some point prior to winding up, a director "knew or ought to have concluded that there was no reasonable prospect that the company would avoid going into insolvent liquidation". Provided that this test is met, the court may, on application by a liquidator, order that a director is liable to contribute to a company's assets. A director's defence, in this circumstance, is that he took every possible step to mitigate potential losses to a company's creditors (see Chapter 15).

REMUNERATION

Directors do not, as a matter of course, receive remuneration for their services, although it is not uncommon for a company's Articles to make provision for the method by which remuneration should be decided (Model Article 19).

APPOINTMENT OF A DIRECTOR

The 2006 Act does not stipulate who is responsible for appointing directors. Guidance is usually provided by a company's Articles (Model Article 17).

The first directors will by notified to the Registrar of Companies on the INO1 Form (2006 Act, s 9(4)(c)), thereafter any additional directors must notify Companies House by completing Form AP01. Any changes to a director's particulars (2006 Act, s 167(1)) must be conveyed by completing Form CH01 within 14 days of the change. All directors must be a least 16 years of age (2006 Act, s 157(1)).

It is important to note that simply being appointed a director of a company does not automatically make a person an employee of the company, although it is possible to be both.

CESSATION OF DIRECTORSHIP

Resignation

It is recognised that directors are free to resign at any time. However, the Articles of a company should be consulted as they generally specify the method of resignation. Model Article 18 provides details of when a directorship must be terminated; circumstances include prohibition by law and physical or mental incapacity. Furthermore, if a director is an employee of a company, their contract of employment should be reviewed to ensure that resignation does not breach any terms of their contract of employment (2006 Act, s 168(5)).

Removal

Irrespective of the Articles of a company, it is possible, for members to remove a director from office by passing an ordinary resolution (2006 Act, s 168(1)). This process can be cumbersome given that special notice requires to be given to a company (2006 Act, ss 312 and s 168(2)), although the Articles may provide for a simplified procedure.

The significance of special notice is intended to highlight to members the significance of the proposed resolution and allow the director in question 28 days (2006 Act, s 312(1)) to prepare any statement they wish to make at the meeting (2006 Act, s 169(2)). This provides the director with the opportunity to bring to the attention of the shareholders any issues surrounding their dismissal. It is debatable how much this protection actually affords a director if the members are resolved to remove him. However, it remains the case that a meeting must be convened (a director cannot be removed by written resolution) and the director has the right to protest.

It is important to note that the Articles cannot circumvent statutory provision, so the right to exercise s 168 of the 2006 Act cannot be removed by a company's Articles. However, a company's Articles must always be referred to as they may confer additional rights to the director being proposed for removal, as was demonstrated in the case of *Bushell v Faith* (1970). A family-run company consisted of two sisters and one brother, each of whom were directors and held 100 shares. The Articles of the company provided that, in the event of an ordinary resolution being proposed at a general meeting to remove a director, the shares held by said director would carry three votes per share instead of one.

The two sisters became unhappy with their brother's involvement in the company and convened a general meeting in line with the legislation in force at the time and passed an ordinary resolution to remove their brother's directorship. Without the weighted voting provision provided for in the Articles, the sisters (holding 200 votes together) could have removed him. However, the brother demanded a poll, in line with the Articles of the company, and defeated the resolution 300 to 200 votes.

The sisters were unhappy with this and successfully petitioned the court, which granted them an injunction. However, the Court of Appeal held that weighted voting rights were acceptable. Companies can amend their Articles by way of special resolution, which provides additional rights or restrictions on particular shares.

Many directors within private companies hold other roles such as shareholder or employee. When this does occur, it is imperative that the individual is fully aware that these are distinct and separate roles within the company. In the case of *Ebrahimi v Westbourne Galleries Ltd and Others* (1972) it is clear what impact the removal of a directorship (in this case due to a division in management within the company) may have on an individual's other interests within a company. From 1945, Shokrollah Ebrahimi ("Ebrahimi") and Asher Nazar Achoury ("Nazar") were carrying on a business in partnership. In 1958 they decided to incorporate a company and transfer their business into the company. Ebrahimi and Nazar were appointed as the first directors and shareholders. Thereafter, Nazar's son George A N Achoury ("George") was appointed as a director and shareholder. As a consequence, Nazar and George together were majority shareholders. Despite being a profitable company, no dividends were ever paid on its shares. However, the three directors did receive remuneration.

In 1969, following a disagreement, Nazar and George passed an ordinary resolution and removed Ebrahimi as a director under s 184 of the Companies Act 1948 ("1948 Act"), which is now s 168 of the 2006 Act. The effect of this meant Ebrahimi was not going to receive any money by way of remuneration. Ebrahimi decided to sever all ties with the company and brought a petition under s 210 of the 1948 Act (now 2006 Act, s 994) that Nazar and George purchase his shares at fair value, failing which he requested that the company be wound up (1948 Act, s 222(f)). Ebrahimi's petition under s 210 of the 1948 Act was unsuccessful as the alleged oppression did not justify such an order. However, the House of Lords held that an order for winding up the company on the basis that it was "just and equitable" should be granted (this would now be under the 1986 Act, s 122(1)(g)). Arguably, Nazar and George could have avoided the winding up of this profitable company by organising an independent valuation of Ebrahimi's shares and then purchasing them.

DISQUALIFICATION OF DIRECTORS

It is possible to become disqualified from holding a directorship under the Company Directors Disqualification Act 1986 ("CDDA 1986"). There are various of grounds where this could occur, including where a person is:

- convicted on indictment in relation to the "promotion, formation, management, liquidation or striking off of a company ..." (CDDA 1986, s 2(1)). This may include a conviction under health and safety legislation, which would fall within the scope of "management";
- continually in breach of the 2006 Act, eg repeated failure to file documents with the Registrar of Companies (CDDA 1986, s 3(1));
- found guilty of fraudulent trading (CDDA 1986, s 4(1)(a)); or
- deemed unfit to be a director of a company (CDDA 1986, ss 6–9).

Essential Facts

- There are various types of directors recognised, other than those formally appointed: for example, *de facto*, shadow, nominee and alternate directors.

- Directors' duties, established at common law, have been codified under ss 171–177 of the 2006 Act. Directors have a duty to act within their powers; to promote the success of the company; to exercise independent judgement; to exercise reasonable care, skill and diligence; to avoid conflicts of interest; not to accept benefits from third parties; and to declare interest in proposed transactions or arrangements.

- A number of remedies are available for a breach of directors' duties under s 178 of the 2006 Act.

- Directors can become personally liable where the "veil of incorporation" is lifted, for example in cases of fraudulent or wrongful trading (1986 Act, ss 213–214).

Essential Cases

Re D'Jan of London Ltd (1993): refers to the level of "care, skill and diligence" that a director must exercise in order to discharge their duty under s 174 of the 2006 Act. The court considered both the objective and subjective test in reaching its conclusion. It concluded, *inter alia*, that where a director is in beach of this duty they may be wholly or partially relieved from their liability if they have acted "honestly and reasonably" (now 2006 Act, s 1157).

Industrial Development Consultants v Cooley (1972): considers a director's duty to avoid a conflict of interest (now 2006 Act, s 175). A former managing director was held accountable to the company for all the benefits, remuneration and fees he personally received under a contract with a third party. He was in a fiduciary relationship with the company and should not benefit personally for knowledge he acquired during that relationship.

Bushell v Faith (1970): refers to the acceptability of weighted voting provision within a company's Articles. Companies are entitled to amend their Articles to provide additional rights or restrictions, provided they do not attempt to circumvent legislation.

Ebrahimi v Westbourne Galleries Ltd and Others (1972): considers the removal of a director by ordinary resolution (now 2006 Act, s 168). This resulted in the company being wound up, as Ebrahimi did not want to remain a shareholder in the company if he no longer had a directorship.

9 CORPORATE KILLING

Arguably one of the most problematic areas of company law is attaching criminal responsibility to a company and its directors. While a company enjoys the status of being a separate legal personality, distinct from its directors and members, it is not a natural person so it is not possible to physically imprison a company. This raises the question: how do you fairly punish a company when a death occurs? Options include:

- *Fine*

  A hefty fine, which may seem appropriate, often negatively impacts on the members of the company, who are often not involved in its management, but they see a reduction in their dividend payments. Moreover, there is always a risk that if the company cannot pay the fine then the business will be unable to sustain itself going forward, and employees will ultimately lose their jobs. While this may be unavoidable in certain cases, arguably it does not punish those who made the decision which resulted in someone's death.

- *Imprisoning directors*

  While it is not possible to imprison a company, it is possible to imprison the directors who are responsible for the running of the company, by lifting the veil of incorporation. However, this approach is not entirely satisfactory given that the director(s) may be unaware of how a particular employee is discharging their role within the company, particularly in large companies. Furthermore, if directors are aware of imprisonment as a potential risk factor in taking up a directorship, individuals may be less inclined to do so. Loss of directors could result in the collapse of the company, which again would have a direct adverse effect on its members and employees rather than those responsible.

Given the inherent problems with punishing a company, why then is it often perceived as an inadequate approach to punish companies under the Health and Safety at Work etc Act 1974 ("1974 Act")? Over the years there have been many successful prosecutions under the 1974 Act, yet publically and politically it does not appear to provide a satisfactory response to a death. When dealing with strict liability crimes the prosecution is not required to prove *mens rea*, which makes successful prosecution somewhat easier, as it is simply sufficient to show that the crime occurred. However, it is intrinsically difficult to deal with crimes of recklessness as no employee would intentionally seek to cause loss of life. However, in certain circumstances this may be the result, as was seen in the case of the Paddington rail disaster, where it was found that driver error was a contributing factor (*Cullen Report*). It is further complicated by the difficulty in trying to establish a "directing mind" (also referred to as the "identification doctrine").

TRANSCO PLC v HM ADVOCATE

The case of *Transco plc* v *HM Advocate* (2004) has historic significance, as it was the first time a company was ever prosecuted for culpable homicide in Scotland. Transco plc was charged following a gas explosion in a private residence in Larkhall, which claimed the life of four members of the Findlay family. It was argued that Transco plc had displayed "a complete and utter disregard for the safety of the public and in particular for the safety of [the four deceased]".

Despite the Crown being unsuccessful in convicting Transco plc under common law, the court ruled that a company could be prosecuted for culpable homicide. No such definitive statement had ever been made until this case, therefore there had been some doubt as to whether a company could actually be convicted of this crime.

The reason the Crown did not achieve a prosecution for culpable homicide was that it failed to identify any one individual who could be described as the "controlling mind" of the company (ie their acts and/ or omissions could be said to be that of the company (the identification doctrine)). To address this failing, the Crown attempted to aggregate the actions of a number of different committees and posts, none of whom could themselves be considered the directing mind unless taken together cumulatively. The court rejected this argument on the basis that the "aggregation principle" was not compatible with either common law or the identification doctrine. Ultimately, Transco plc was successfully fined under the 1974 Act.

POST-TRANSCO

While the case of Transco plc did provide clarity on the possibility of a company facing charges of culpable homicide, it did raise a number of issues, including the following:

- Are smaller companies unfairly prejudiced? Clearly, it is easier to identify the "directing mind" within a small company, compared to a larger company with many tiers of management.

- By specifically rejecting the use of the aggregation principle, the longer a company suffers from ineffective management, the harder it will be to achieve a prosecution.

- The highlighting of the difficulty the Crown faces under common law, which requires the establishment of *mens rea*. Clearly this is intrinsically more difficult to prove in relation to a corporate vehicle as opposed to a human being.

- Why it is not possible for an employer to be held vicariously liable for a common law crime.

- At common law the Crown enjoys immunity from prosecution.

Clearly, the position was seen as unacceptable and required greater clarity, particularly in Scotland, with the greatest mortality and serious injury rates in the whole of the United Kingdom. Karen Gillon (MSP) introduced a Private Member's Bill, the Culpable Homicide (Scotland) Bill, in June 2006, with the aim of rectifying the position. The Bill did not progress due to lack of support and there was, *inter alia*, concern about having a different approach to corporate prosecution north and south of the Border.

THE CORPORATE MANSLAUGHTER AND CORPORATE HOMICIDE ACT 2007

The Corporate Manslaughter and Corporate Homicide Act 2007 ("2007 Act") is applicable to the United Kingdom, with the aim of holding corporate vehicles accountable. It specifically addresses some of the problems which arise in the prosecution of corporate entities at common law.

Who can face prosecution under the 2007 Act?

One of the objectives of the 2007 Act is to focus on corporate vehicles, such as companies and partnerships. However, some governmental bodies are caught within its scope, including the following:

- centrally – the Ministry of Defence, the Scottish Office, and the Department of Health (2007 Act, Sch 1);
- regionally – local authorities and police forces (2007 Act, s 13).

Clearly, a number of significant restrictions and indeed exemptions arise regarding any prosecutions of these departments. Similar types of limitation exist in relation to the Crown, which has now seen the removal of its blanket protection.

What is the new offence?

A company (2007 Act, s 1(2) and Sch 1 details all bodies covered) will be guilty of corporate homicide where there has been a death, which was caused by "a gross breach of a relevant duty of care" (2007 Act, s 1(1)(b)). However, the guilt of a company can be established only if an element of the breach relates to the way in which the company's "activities are managed or organised" (2007 Act, s 1(1)).

Consequently, where a death has occurred there are three essential elements to the offence which must be considered in turn.

(i) Was there a "gross breach"?

If it can be established that a relevant duty of care is owed, it is then for a jury to determine whether there has been a gross breach of that duty (2007 Act, s 8(1)). An act or omission by the company will be deemed "a 'gross' breach if the conduct alleged to amount to a breach of that duty falls far below what can reasonably be expected ... in the circumstances" (2007 Act, s 1(4)(b)).

The 2007 Act provides guidance on this and includes the following:

- whether the company complied with all relevant health and safety legislation associated with the breach and the extent of any contravention (2007 Act, s 8(2)); and
- consideration of the internal procedures, policies, systems and accepted practices implemented within the company in relation to health and safety. Where a death occurs it will be difficult to secure a conviction under the 2007 Act if the management within the company has made and implemented reasonable health and safety provisions (2007 Act, s 8).

(ii) Did a "relevant duty of care" exist?

Pursuant to s 2 of the 2007 Act (partially in force), an offence may only be committed by a company where they owe a "relevant duty of care". This new offence does not create new duties of care that were not previously owed under the law of negligence. The duty of care under s 2(1) of the 2007 Act exists in many forms and includes a duty:

- "to its employees or to other persons working" for the company, including provision of a safe system of work;
- where the company provides goods and/or services (eg to its clients/ customers); and
- as an "occupier of premises" and land (ie they must be maintained in a safe manner).

If it can be established that a relevant duty of care is owed by the company to the victim, then the breach must correlate to how the activities of the company are internally managed, and this management failure must amount to a "substantial element" of the breach (2007 Act, s 1(3)), which resulted in the death. Therefore, it is imperative to consider the position of senior management.

(iii) Did the role of "senior management" significantly contribute to the death?

The 2007 Act does not identify a specific tier of management that would be categorised as "senior management" (2007 Act, s 1(4)(c)), therefore those who fall within this group will vary significantly between companies. However, they must be individuals who have significant roles in either: (i) making decisions about how a company's activities will be managed or organised; or (ii) being involved in the actual management or organising of activities (2007 Act, s 1(4)(c)).

Undoubtedly, the difficulty will be in establishing if the role of senior management was a significant contributing factor in the death. This will depend on the company and is decided after consideration of the facts and who had control or influence over their procedures and employees. Members of senior management are not responsible for the actions of their staff who act in a reckless or unpredictable manner.

Exempt categories

For the sake of completeness, it is important to be aware that there are some exemption provisions, although they apply to public authorities. It was deemed necessary to have a number of general and specific limitations. Consequently, a number of duties have been removed from the classification of a "relevant duty of care" (2007 Act, s 3).

Penalties

It is important to remember that this piece of legislation applies to organisations (2007 Act, s 1(2)), so an individual cannot be found to be in breach of the 2007 Act. Furthermore, a human person "cannot be guilty of aiding, abetting, counselling or procuring, or being art and part in, the commission of an offence of corporate homicide" (2007 Act, s 18(2)). Consequently, the 2007 Act does not increase a director's exposure to liability; they remain open to prosecution both at common law and under the relevant health and safety legislation.

Any breach of the 2007 Act can only be prosecuted under indictment in the High Court of Justiciary (2007 Act, s 1(7)). While the court cannot imprison a company, a fine may be imposed (no maximum limit is set down in the 2007 Act). In addition to a fine, it is possible for the court to impose on a company the following sanctions:

- *Remedial orders*
  Pursuant to s 9 of the 2007 Act, this order would require the company to undertake a number of steps to rectify its practices, which the court believes, *inter alia*, may remedy the breach, or contributed to the breach by way of deficient internal health and safety policies and procedures. The court will specify a time limit for the company to fulfil these requirements. Failure to comply with a remedial order may result in conviction and fine.

- *Publicity orders*
  The court may require a company to put details of the crime into the public arena, including details of the breach, the amount of the fine and the particulars of any remedial order imposed. Again, failure to comply will result in an additional conviction on indictment and a fine (2007 Act, s 10).

Defence

When a company faces prosecution under the 2007 Act, they may be able to successfully defend their position by demonstrating that they have adequate health and safety procedures and policies in place.

It is possible for a fatality to occur but the liability to be significantly different, eg where a sole trader and a company are both carrying on the exact same business. While both are subject to prosecution under the 1974 Act and common law, provided all the necessary criteria are met, only the company may additionally be prosecuted under the 2007 Act.

Essential Facts

- Key legislation – the Corporate Manslaughter and Corporate Homicide Act 2007.
- The 2007 Act only applies to organisations, so an individual cannot be prosecuted for a breach of the legislation.
- The 2007 Act introduces a new offence whereby a company can be found guilty of corporate homicide where a death has occurred as a result of a "gross breach of a relevant duty of care" and where the breach is related to how a company's "activities are managed".
- Provided that the management of a company implements appropriate health and safety policies, procedures and systems it will be difficult to secure a prosecution under the 2007 Act where a death occurs.
- Penalties for a successful prosecution under the 2007 Act include remedial and publicity orders.

Essential Case

Transco plc v HM Advocate (2004): is a historic Scottish case which established definitively that a company could be prosecuted for culpable homicide. Ultimately, the Crown was successful only in securing a prosecution under the 1974 Act, as it was unable to establish a "directing mind" within the company.

10 MEMBERSHIP

Pursuant to s 123(1) of the Companies Act 2006 ("2006 Act"), a company is required to have the minimum of one person as a shareholder, at any one time. Given the contractual nature of membership, restrictions exist in relation to certain individuals becoming members of a company: for example, individuals who lack legal capacity, who are of unsound mind or who have been declared bankrupt.

Provided a person is not restricted from being a shareholder and they agree to membership, there are several ways for a person to become a member of a company, including the following:

* subscription to a company's memorandum of association ("Memorandum") (2006 Act, s 8);

* being allotted shares (2006 Act, ss 549–551);

* receiving a transfer of shares from an existing member, guidance can be found in article 26 (SI 2008/3229) ("Model Articles") of a company's Articles of Association ("the Articles"); or

* receiving a transmission of shares (Model Article 27), which occurs on the bankruptcy or death of a member and results in the transmission of their shares to a trustee or personal representative.

Membership exists only once a person's name and details have been recorded in a company's register of members (2006 Act, s 127). Ordinarily, once registered, a company would then issue a share certificate to a member detailing their shareholding (Model Article 24).

DIVIDENDS

Members often receive dividends on the shares they hold, although there is no automatic right to this. Directors of a company recommend the amount of dividend that should be paid on a share, and the members then pass an ordinary resolution declaring that dividend (Model Article 30). Dividends are paid from a company's distributable profits (2006 Act, s 830) either by way of cash or company asset (Model Article 34) (see Chapter 12).

LIABILITY

A member's liability will be detailed in the Memorandum of a company (2006 Act, s 9(2)(c)). Generally, a member is liable to pay to a company the full nominal value (and any agreed share premium) on all the shares held and registered in their name.

RIGHTS

A company's constitution provides a membership contract between a company and its members (2006 Act, s 33). Consequently, where resolutions are passed at general meetings (or by written resolution), all members of a company are bound by the decision, whether or not they personally vote in favour of passing the said resolutions.

Foss v Harbottle (1843)

Historically, the principle of majority rule was expounded in the case of *Foss* v *Harbottle* (see Chapter 11), which involved minority shareholders attempting to bring a case, on behalf of the company, alleging that the majority shareholders sold to the company a piece of land at an over-inflated price. The court held, *inter alia*, that the company alone was the "proper plaintiff". This decision has subsequently, in part, been viewed as unacceptable. *Foss* gave no consideration to the fact that it was the majority shareholders themselves who were responsible for the excessive price being paid by the company, yet it was their approval that was required in order to pursue an action (which in the circumstances was unlikely). Thereafter, the courts recognised a number of exceptions to the rules laid down in *Foss* and only if minority members could fall within these exceptions could they raise an action. However, now under the 2006 Act they have new legislative protection in the shape of derivative proceedings (2006 Act, ss 265–269 – see Chapter 11).

Legislative protection

In addition to derivative proceedings (2006 Act, ss 265–269), minority members may make a petition to the court under s 994 of the 2006 Act, alleging unfair prejudice in relation to the past or present acts or omissions of a company, which affect the members as a whole, or some group of them. If satisfied, the court may order such relief as it deems appropriate: for example, requiring that the majority members of the company purchase the minority members' shares, at a fair value (2006 Act, s 996) (see Chapter 11).

Alternatively, minority members may petition the court for a company to be wound up, based on the "just and equitable" principle under s 122(1)(g) of the Insolvency Act 1986. The courts will usually only consider this type of petition in circumstances where no other option is available (see Chapter 11).

CESSATION OF MEMBERSHIP

An individual's membership ceases when it is documented in a company's register of members. This can occur in a variety of circumstances, including on the transfer or transmission of shares.

SHARE CAPITAL

Maintaining share capital

The issued share capital of a company may be viewed as a fund available to creditors of a company. As a result, companies are prohibited from issuing shares at less than their nominal value (2006 Act, s 542) and any premium paid on a share must be deposited into a separate share premium account, which is non-distributable. Certain legislative provisions are designed to protect a company's capital, including regulating its reduction (2006 Act, s 641) and the purchase of its own shares (2006 Act, s 690) (see Chapter 12).

Altering share capital

The share capital of a company may be altered, if the necessary authorisation is provided in its Articles. A company may only alter its share capital as stipulated in s 617 of the 2006 Act, which includes:

- increasing its share capital by the creation of new shares;
- reducing its share capital (2006 Act, s 641);
- consolidation or sub-division of all or part of the existing share capital into shares with an increased or decreased nominal value;
- reconversion of stock into shares; and
- redomination of all or part of its shares.

When altering the share capital of a company it may be necessary to pass a resolution (2006 Act, ss 618(3) and 620(2)) and any alteration requires that the necessary forms are filed with the Registrar of Companies within

1 month from the date of the resolution (2006 Act, ss 619, 621 and 689) (see Chapter 12).

Allotting shares

In order for a company to allot shares, directors must have the necessary authority, pursuant to ss 549–551 of the 2006 Act; this may be provided for in a company's Articles or can be provided by its members by the passing of a resolution. Where directors have been provided with authorisation (may be general authorisation and could be conditional or unconditional) to allot shares it must specify the following:

• maximum number of shares which may be allotted;
• a date for expiry of the authorisation (the date cannot exceed 5 years).

The authorisation provided by the company may be renewed, revoked or varied by the passing of a further resolution. Failure to have the necessary authority will result in a director facing criminal sanctions, but will not invalidate the allotment.

Statutory pre-emption rights exist in relation to the issue of new shares (2006 Act, s 561) in a company. This means that a company must first offer to the existing shareholders the new issue of shares, in proportion to their existing shareholding. This provision is designed to prevent the dilution of existing members' rights with the issue of new shares.

The offer of new shares to existing members must be made in writing and is open for acceptance for a minimum of 14 days (2006 Act, s 562). This pre-emption right may be disapplied under ss 569–571 of the 2006 Act. If the shares are not taken up by the current members or they waive their pre-emption rights, the new shares can be offered to third parties. Once the shares have been allotted, a company's register of members should be updated and a share certificate issued in respect of the newly allotted shares (2006 Act, s 769(1)).

Any allotment of shares which contravenes s 561 of the 2006 Act does not invalidate the allotment; however, every officer who permitted the allotment will be liable jointly and severally to compensate any shareholder who should have been offered the new shares (2006 Act, s 563(2)).

Transferring shares

The transfer of shares is generally undertaken voluntarily and in accordance with the company's Articles (2006 Act, s 544(1)). However, circumstances can arise where there is a compulsory transfer of shares, for example on insolvency, death or termination of employment.

Unlike with the allotment of shares, statutory pre-emption rights do not exist in relation to the transfer of shares, although it is not uncommon for a company's Articles to contain pre-emption rights. The Model Articles do not provide such provision; however, Model Article 26 provides that the directors of a company have the power to refuse to register the transfer of shares.

On the transfer of shares a company must have delivered to it an instrument of transfer duly signed and stamped (ie a stock transfer form). Stamp duty is payable at half a per cent of the total consideration payable (rounded up to the nearest £5) (Finance Act 1999, s 112)), although certain transfers are totally or partially exempt from this duty. Again, a share certificate will be issued to the transferee, and the register of members will be amended accordingly.

Essential Facts

- Membership exists only when a person's name is entered into a company's register of members.
- A subscriber's liability is detailed in a company's Memorandum.
- A company's constitution provides a membership contract between a company and its members (2006 Act, s 33).
- Members enjoy a variety of legislative protection, including bringing derivative proceedings (2006 Act, ss 265–269), or a petition for unfair prejudice (2006 Act, ss 994–996).
- Maintenance of a company's share capital is important; consequently, statutory safeguards exist.
- To alter a company's share capital, a resolution must be passed and filed with the Registrar of Companies.
- Companies must have authority to allot shares (2006 Act, ss 549–551) and statutory pre-emption rights exist (2006 Act, s 561).
- Share transfers are usually voluntary, and no statutory pre-emption rights exist.

Essential Cases

Foss v Harbottle (1843): refers to the principle of majority rule. In circumstances where an alleged wrong has been done to a company, minority shareholders cannot bring an action on behalf of the company. A company is a distinct legal entity and, therefore, the "proper plaintiff". It is now judicially accepted that there are certain exceptions to this principle.

11 MAJORITY RULE AND MINORITY PROTECTION

The Articles of Association and the Companies Act 2006 reserve to the members the power to make the most important constitutional changes. Most decisions are made by majority vote. Usually, the members of the company have to live with the outcome, no matter how much some of them may be unhappy with it, and did not vote for it. This is the same in any democratic system of decision-making. As seen in Chapter 7, generally in a company limited by shares, voting is by show of hands or by a poll, which takes account of the number of shares held by each member. In other types of company, members would generally have one vote each. Most decisions call for a particular majority vote, either a simple majority or a three-quarters majority – for example, removal of a director calls for a simple majority vote (ordinary resolution) under s 168 of the Companies Act 2006, while altering the Articles of Association calls for a three-quarters majority vote (special resolution) under s 21 of the Companies Act 2009. Generally, where constitutional changes have to be made by the members, they are proposed by the board of directors. Problems can arise in those companies where some members hold more than 75 per cent of the vote and particularly where the board of directors itself owns or controls more than 75 per cent of the vote. In these instances, there is scope for the majority to treat the company as if it were entirely theirs to do with as they wish. Because of this, there are some statutory rights and remedies available to the minority, which will be discussed in this chapter.

THE PRINCIPLE OF MAJORITY RULE

This is a rule that comes from the case law. It states that when a wrong has been done to a company, it is for the company itself as a legal person to take action. The court would usually refuse to hear a case brought by a member or minority members, seeking a remedy for the company. The leading case that expressed this principle is *Foss* v *Harbottle* (1843). In this case, minority shareholders brought an action on behalf of the company against its directors, alleging that they had defrauded the company, and seeking an order calling for them to make good the company's alleged losses. The court refused, on the grounds that only the company could sue, and, as the company and its board of directors were still in existence, there was nothing to stop it calling a general meeting and bringing an action itself.

There are various justifications for this rule: (i) the company is a legal person and is therefore the proper pursuer; (ii) if a wrong is capable of being ratified by the company, it is illogical to allow a minority to raise an action if the wrong might cease to be so if ratified; (iii) the courts do not wish to open the floodgates to numerous identical actions brought by different minority members on the same matters.

However, even early on, some exceptions to the rule were recognised by the courts, with minority members being allowed to raise actions for the benefit of the company when the majority would not do so. These included acts that were incapable of ratification because they were *ultra vires* the company or illegal. There were some other exceptions too.

The derivative action under the Companies Act 2006

In order to be allowed to bring a case to court under one of the exceptions to *Foss* v *Harbottle*, the case had to fit one of the categories of exceptions recognised in the case law. This was very difficult, especially in Scotland, because of a scarcity of cases, which made the law very uncertain. For example, if the wrong involved negligence on the part of the directors, there was uncertainty about whether or not a derivative action could be brought. Therefore the law was reformed in the Companies Act 2006, which created a new statutory form of derivative action, replacing the old common law exceptions, with different rules for Scotland from those applying to England and Wales and Northern Ireland because of different rules of court procedure. The rules for Scotland are in ss 265–269.

Under ss 265–269, a member or members of a company may raise derivative proceedings in the name of the company to protect the interests of the company and obtain a remedy on its behalf, in a case where any actual or proposed act or omission involves negligence, default, breach of duty or breach of trust by a director or directors of the company. Any remedy granted by the court (such as damages) would go to the company and not the applicant personally.

The leave of the court must first be obtained before proceedings can be brought. At the very least, the court must be persuaded that there is a *prima facie* case, or it must refuse the application. There are various procedural hurdles that must be satisfied, otherwise leave to bring the case must be refused under s 268(1):

- the case must be one that a director acting in accordance with his duty to promote the success of the company for the benefit if its members would consider worth raising;
- the act or omission complained of must not be one that has been authorised by the company or ratified by it after the event.

Other factors set out in s 268(2) that the court must take into account before deciding whether to allow the case to proceed are:

- whether the applicant is acting in good faith;
- the degree of importance that a director complying with his duty would attach to the raising of this action;
- in relation to acts or omissions that have not yet occurred, whether they would be likely to be authorised by the company or ratified after the event;
- in relation to acts that have occurred, whether the act would be likely to be ratified;
- whether the company has decided not to raise proceedings;
- whether the member would have other personal remedies.

Section 268(3) states that the court should also take into account the views of other members of the company who do not have a personal interest in the case.

Procedurally, there are two stages in deciding whether leave to bring the case should be allowed: at the first stage the court considers the application and the evidence, and must refuse it if it does not disclose a *prima facie* case. The next stage occurs after service of court papers, to which the company is invited. These procedural stages are intended to sift out unmeritorious cases.

Since these sections came into force, some case law is beginning to emerge in Scotland. In *Wishart, Petitioner* (2010) a minority shareholder petitioned the court for an order under s 266 of the Companies Act 2006 for leave to bring an action in the name of the company against a shareholder/director of the company and also against another company owned by him on the ground that business had been diverted to that other company and the other company had knowingly received the proceeds. At first instance the Lord Ordinary had allowed a hearing to go ahead as to whether there was a *prima facie* case and granted an order to indemnify the petitioner for expenses, though there was no provision for this in the legislation or the rules of court, in contrast to the English rules. The respondent reclaimed on the basis that the petitioner should have to prove more than a *prima facie* case under s 266, that the petitioner could have used another remedy such as a petition on the basis of suffering unfair prejudice (see later in this chapter), and that s 266 did not permit the court to oblige the company to indemnify the petitioner for expenses. The Inner House held that the court did have to consider the merits of the case in outline in order to decide whether it should be allowed to proceed, and, provided the matters in s 268(1) were met and the matters in s 268(2) were taken into account, the decision to grant leave to allow the case to be brought was a matter for the decision of the court. The Inner House also held that, although the petitioner could have petitioned the court alleging unfair prejudice, that would be an indirect means to an end, and using s 266 was competent. Also, the issue of the award of an indemnity for expenses, though not provided for explicitly in the legislation, was within the court's powers and was construed as being Parliament's intention when enacting these provisions, as leave to bring the case is needed in Scotland and not in England, and it could not have been Parliament's intention for a petitioner to be out of pocket personally when seeking a remedy for a company. After a further appeal, a prospective order for expenses was granted, covering the derivative action and the application, which was subject to modification depending on possible material change in the company's circumstances in future.

A personal remedy

Section 265(6) states that ss 266–269 do not change any rules under which a member can raise proceedings against a company seeking a personal remedy for an act or omission done by the directors of the company affecting the member personally. This leaves intact previous case law which would allow such a remedy. One such case is *Pender* v *Lushington* (1877) in which nominee shareholders to whom shares had been validly transferred were not allowed to vote, because the directors saw this as a device to get round constitutional limits on the upper number of votes per member in the company. The court held that the nominee shareholders should have been allowed to vote. Such a case could also probably also be brought as an unfair prejudice case (see below).

Unfairly prejudicial conduct

This remedy has been found in some form in statutory law since the Companies Act 1948, which previously included the right to petition for a remedy where a member had suffered "oppressive" conduct at the hands of a company. That provision was rarely successful, as oppressive conduct was interpreted very strictly. The current provision was introduced in 1980, although it has been amended slightly over the years. It is now found in ss 994–999 of the Companies Act 2006 and the same rules apply to England and Wales, Northern Ireland and Scotland.

Section 994 allows a member or members to petition the court for an order on the grounds that the affairs of the company are being or have been conducted in a manner that is unfairly prejudicial to the interests of some or all of its members including at least himself. This specifically includes removal of the auditor on the grounds of divergence of opinion on accounting or auditing matters.

If the petition is successful, the remedies under s 996 include:

- an order regulating the affairs of the company in the future;
- an order requiring the company to refrain from doing something (interdict) or to do an act that it has omitted to do;
- an order authorising the bringing of civil proceedings in the name of the company;
- an order forbidding alterations of the Articles of Association to be made without the court's permission;
- an order providing for the purchase of shares of any member of the company (usually the petitioner) by other members or by the company itself, and, if by the company, for the reduction in capital of the company.

An order for the purchase of shares is the order that is generally sought. This is particularly useful in small private companies where there is no market for shares outside the company. The court may be asked to determine the valuation, which may be discounted to reflect the fact that it is a minority shareholding. However, in view of the fact that the minority is usually an unwilling seller, often the court does not apply a discount. The valuation put on the shares can also reflect the part played by the petitioner in the destruction of the relationship between the parties. The issue of valuation may be a difficult one, as both sides may have radically different views reflecting entrenched positions caused by the breakdown in their relationship.

Apart from the orders listed in s 996, other court orders would also be competent.

In *Robertson, Petitioner (No 1)* (2009) the Court of Session approved a deduction of losses made on foreign exchange contracts to be made from the respondent's half share which the court had ordered was to be bought by the petitioner, to reflect the fact that the respondent had excluded the petitioner from any knowledge that the company had been engaging in foreign exchange dealing, rather than scrap metal dealing as he thought.

In *West Coast Capital (LIOS) Ltd, Petitioners* (2008) the Court of Session was asked by West Coast Capital, a minority shareholder in Dobbies Garden Centres plc to grant an interim interdict to prevent Dobbies putting a resolution to its Annual General Meeting to allot new shares to provide funds for expansion. The Outer House of the Court of Session refused to grant this interim order, for lack of evidence at that early point in the proceedings (before all the evidence had been heard) as to whether the order would unfairly harm the company or unfairly benefit the petitioner who also had interests in a rival company.

A great many cases have been brought under the statutory unfair prejudice provisions, which have been judicially interpreted. It was held in *Re Saul Harrison & Sons plc* (1995) that, to have a case, the conduct complained of must be both unfair *and* prejudicial. As Neill LJ stated:

> "The words 'unfairly prejudicial' are general words and they should be applied flexibly to meet the circumstances of the particular case ... The conduct must be both prejudicial (in the sense of causing prejudice or harm to the relevant interests) and also unfairly so: conduct may be unfair without being prejudicial or prejudicial without being unfair, and it is not sufficient if the conduct satisfies only one of these tests."

In *Re Bovey Hotel Ventures Ltd* (1981) the court held that the test of unfairly prejudicial conduct is concerned with the effect of the conduct on the petitioner and not the motive behind it: it was not necessary for the petitioner to prove that the person whose conduct was complained of knew they were acting unfairly or whether they were acting in bad faith. The test was whether a reasonable bystander, observing the consequences of the conduct, would regard the conduct as substantially prejudicing the petitioner's interests.

Although good faith on the part of the petitioner is a factor that the court has to take into account when there is a petition under s 266 (the new derivative action, discussed above) it is not a requirement in an unfair prejudice petition. In *Re London School of Electronics Ltd* (1986) the relationship broke down between the petitioner, who was a part shareholder in the London School of Electronics ("the School"), and two individuals who owned another company which owned the rest of the shares in the School. The petitioner was dismissed as a director and all parties resorted to dirty tricks such as recruiting the students of the School to rival institutions. Although the petitioner's own behaviour had not been without fault, the court held that was not a bar to the court's granting a remedy, although it might have a bearing on the relief the court might be prepared to grant.

If the petitioner could have done more to protect his position without resorting to an unfair prejudice petition, the court may refuse to grant a remedy. In *Re R A Noble & Sons (Clothing) Ltd* (1983) the petitioner was a director/shareholder who took very little interest in the company's affairs and later petitioned the court seeking relief on the grounds of unfair prejudice because he had been sidelined. The court refused because he could have remedied his situation by attending board meetings and general meetings.

In some small private companies, there is particular potential for unfair prejudice to arise where all the shares are held by a few individuals who are also the only directors. In such cases, the majority of directors/shareholders can gang up against one of their number and remove him or her from office by ordinary resolution under s 168 of the Companies Act 2006. In this kind of company it may be that none of the other directors/shareholders or the company itself is willing to buy the shares. It is also likely that no dividend is paid on the shares. This means that the director has been ousted but his shares are locked in the company without any benefit to the former director. In such cases, the courts have sometimes allowed a petition to be brought by the former director seeking an order for the company or one of the other shareholders to buy the shares. This is justified on the basis that it will be allowed where the company is a quasi-partnership, where either the parties were formerly in partnership and then formed a company, or the relationship within the company is run on informal lines and not in strict accordance with the Articles of Association. In such a case the court may be prepared to recognise that the petitioner has a legitimate expectation as a shareholder in such a company of being able to take part in the management of the company, and, if deprived of that right, can petition the court on the ground of unfair prejudice. One such case was *Re London School of Electronics Ltd*, mentioned above. However, as shown in *Re Astec (BSR) plc* (1998), this approach will never be recognised as applying to listed public companies, which have to be assumed to be run strictly in accordance with their Articles of Association, and where, of course, any director/shareholder who is ousted from his directorship would be able to sell his shares on a public market.

The limits of the notion of legitimate expectations were considered by the House of Lords in *O'Neill* v *Phillips* (1999), and received a restricted interpretation. Phillips had been the sole shareholder and director in a small company that specialised in the removal of asbestos from buildings.

O'Neill, one of the employees, had impressed Phillips, who arranged for O'Neill to receive 25 per cent of the shares and to become a director, with talk of O'Neill taking over the management of the business and receiving 50 per cent of the profits. Although there was no formal undertaking to pay O'Neill 50 per cent of the profits, Phillips did do so, and retired, leaving O'Neill as the sole director. The company was hit by a recession in the early 1990s, at which point Phillips took back the management of the company and O'Neill was relegated to being the manager of the German branch of the company, and no longer received 50 per cent of the profits. The relations between the two men broke down and O'Neill took steps towards setting up a rival business. O'Neill petitioned the court on the grounds of unfair prejudice, claiming that he had had a legitimate expectation to receive an allocation of shares to give him 50 per cent of the profits, which had not been honoured, and sought to have his 25 per cent holding purchased. Phillips had already made an offer to do so, which had been rejected. There was evidence that O'Neill had supported the business by mortgaging his house to support a personal guarantee for bank borrowings. The House of Lords held that unfairness had not been established in the absence of an agreed term in the Articles of Association that the shares would be repurchased, and that there had never been a contractual agreement to give a 50 per cent shareholding to O'Neill. The House of Lords held that the concept of fairness was context-dependent. Companies were set up with some formality and the normal expectation is that they will be run in accordance with their Articles of Association and any shareholders' agreements. However, as company law developed from the law of partnership, the principle of good faith that applies in partnership applies also in company law, as reflected in the "just and equitable" ground of liquidation, discussed later in this chapter. The House of Lords recognised that unfairness in particular cases might arise either where the rules are breached, or where they are used in a manner that contravenes good faith.

In *O'Neill* v *Phillips* the court set limits to the expansion of the concept of legitimate expectations and also held that there was no right of "no fault divorce" for shareholders who fall out with their companies, apart from exceptional cases where equitable principles so demand (such as quasi-partnership companies where one shareholder/director is removed as a director, as discussed above). Before the Companies Act 2006 was enacted, considerable preliminary work was done to explore the impact of possible reforms. One suggested reform was to provide for an exit article to be put into Articles of Association, providing for a director/shareholder of a small private company to have a right to be bought out if the relationship between the parties comes to an end. However, this was not enacted, and there was a realisation that the economic impact of such an article might be to lead to the unnecessary insolvency of very small companies and their remaining shareholders.

Successful unfair prejudice petitions have been brought by minority shareholders on the basis of serious breach of directors' duties. One such case is *Re McCarthy Surfacing Ltd* (2008) in which a petition was brought by three shareholders who were former managers and who had already lost an earlier unfair prejudice petition. The evidence was that the directors took 81 per cent of the profits personally as bonus payments, caused the company to do deals with the managing director without checking whether the prices paid were reasonable, and did not pay a dividend when the company could have done so. The court held that breaches of directors' duties were established, and ordered the purchase of the petitioners' shares by the remaining directors/shareholders at a price to be fixed by the court.

In *Re D & R Chemicals Ltd* (1989) where the majority shareholder arranged for the company to issue more shares to himself, so that his majority holding of 60 per cent became 96 per cent (which would allow the majority to pass special resolutions), the court held that this dilution of the minority's stake in the company was unfairly prejudicial.

Depending on the circumstances of the company and its shareholders, in some cases the court has ordered the minority shareholder to buy out the majority shareholder, rather than ordering the company itself or the majority shareholder to buy out the minority. This was done in *Re Brenfield Squash Racquets Club Ltd* (1996) and also *Robertson, Petitioner (No 1)* (2009) mentioned above, in which shares were held 50/50 between the petitioner and the two respondents.

A recent Scottish case, which shows how an unfair prejudice petition can be used where the relationship between the parties has broken down, is *Fowler* v *Gruber* (2009). The company had been founded by Fowler, although he could not initially become involved in it because of a restrictive covenant from a former employment. Shares were held for him by Gruber while a third person initially acted as managing director, a position later taken on by Gruber, who also bought that person's shares, financed by a loan from the company which was later written off, making him the majority shareholder. Gruber did later repay that loan on being advised that it was illegal. Fowler petitioned the court on the ground of unfair prejudice, claiming that Gruber was taking excessive remuneration from the company and had prevented Fowler from examining the financial position of the company. Fowler sought either to be appointed as a director by Gruber or to have his shareholding purchased at a fair price by the company. The court found that, although the company could not have employed Fowler for some years for financial reasons, even after the restrictive covenant had come to an end, he had been excluded from management for some years after that; the loan by the company to Gruber to enable him to buy shares was unfairly prejudicial; and Gruber's remuneration package was excessive; therefore, as it would not be sensible for Fowler to be appointed a director, as Gruber would have the power as a majority shareholder to remove him, the best course of action was to grant an order for the purchase of Fowler's shares at a valuation set by the court, which included a discount for its being a minority shareholding.

The new derivative action or an unfair prejudice petition?

If the issue is that a minority shareholder seeks a remedy for the company caused by breach of directors' duties, the shareholder may have a choice between the new derivative action and an unfair prejudice petition in which the remedy sought is authority to raise an action in the name of the company. Once all the uncertainties in the procedure in ss 266–269 of the Companies Act 2006 are eventually clarified as cases come before the courts, and now that there is some clarification in Scotland of the fact that the petitioner can be indemnified for his expenses from the company, that remedy may be more used than in the past.

Double counting (reflective loss)

If a shareholder is successful in obtaining a remedy for a company, the court will not let that shareholder also seek a personal remedy if that would amount to his obtaining a personal remedy that is merely reflective of the company's loss, as that would allow the shareholder to recover more than once for the same loss, in that the share price would be expected to recover on receipt by the company of an award of damages. In *Johnson* v *Gore Wood (No 1)* (2002), a company had obtained a substantial settlement out of court in a negligence case against its solicitors over a property purchase, in which it had had to sue the seller before obtaining title to the property, during which time the company had suffered severe financial hardship, as had Johnson, one of its shareholders. Johnson then sued the solicitors in his personal capacity, and the House of Lords recognised that some of what he sued for was not reflective loss, including the cost of his having to borrow at high rates of interest, and the fact that he had lost his shareholding in the company because he had had to transfer it to a lender.

The appointment of a judicial factor

In Scotland the court can appoint a judicial factor to be an interim manager. This can be useful if a company is in complete disarray: for example, if it has no directors at all, as was the case with the department store company Bremners in *Weir* v *Rees* (1991). The appointment of a judicial factor provided essential management for this company, in which there were warring factions and all the directors had been removed from office, to enable a general meeting to be held to appoint fresh directors.

WINDING UP A COMPANY ON THE "JUST AND EQUITABLE" GROUND

Ultimately, if an unhappy minority member cannot resolve matters any other way, the remedy of last resort is to petition the court to put the company into liquidation on the ground that it is just and equitable to do so. This statutory remedy is found in s 122(1)(g) of the Insolvency Act 1986, and the same rules apply in Scotland as in England and Wales, but not to Northern Ireland.

There are restrictions on the availability of liquidation on this ground, to ensure that it is not abused. First, it is awarded at the discretion of the court and not as of right. Second, where a shareholder petitions, his shares must have been held for 6 out of the past 18 months, or have been inherited, or have been acquired directly from the company. This is to prevent shares being purchased just for the purpose of seeking to have the company wound up. Third, except where a member would be liable as a contributory in the liquidation of a company, the company must be solvent if it is to be wound up by a member on this ground, to ensure that there would be some financial benefit accruing to the member and that the purpose of the petition is not just bloody-mindedness. Also, the court will not wind up a company on this ground if it appears to the court that there is another remedy which it would be reasonable to expect the petitioner to use (such as a petition on the ground of unfair prejudice). Finally, the words "just and equitable" have not been defined in the Insolvency Act 1986, and have been applied flexibly by the courts. It appears that the petitioner must be acting in good faith.

In some cases a member makes two separate petitions: one claiming unfairly prejudicial conduct under s 994 of the Companies Act 2006; and another seeking a winding up order on the "just and equitable" ground under s 122(1)(g) of the Insolvency Act 1986, an example being *Jesner* v *Jarrad Properties Ltd* (1994), which is discussed in the next paragraph.

As might be expected, there are relatively few cases where companies are wound up on the "just and equitable" ground, as it is not economically sensible to wind up profitable companies if another solution can be found. However, in small quasi-partnership companies where the relationship between the shareholders and directors has irretrievably broken down, and it is not obvious who should buy out whom, it may offer the best solution. In *Jesner* v *Jarrad Properties Ltd* (1994) two family companies, Jesner and Sons Ltd ("Jesner") and Jarrad Properties Ltd ("Jarrad"), had been run informally for the benefit of members of the Jesner family. At times, one company supported the other with loans, and later on this was reversed. Eventually, two members of the Jesner family sought an order for the purchase of their shares on the basis of unfairly prejudicial conduct relating to the granting of a security by Jarrad in breach of its constitution and the granting of interest-free loans to Jesner. They also sought liquidation of the company on the "just and equitable" ground. The sheriff court had refused the petition relating to unfairly prejudicial conduct, as the evidence showed that the fact that the two companies had been run in an informal manner together had been done in good faith and was therefore not unfair. However, on appeal, the Inner House of the Court of Session again refused the petition based on unfair prejudice, but did grant the winding-up order, on the ground that there had been loss of confidence in the way the company was being run.

Todd v *Todd* (2008) is a recent Scottish case demonstrating that winding up on the "just and equitable" ground will be granted in appropriate cases. The case concerned a family company that ran various nursing homes. Mr and Mrs Todd split up, after which Mr Todd and other directors misappropriated a large sum of the company's money. Mrs Todd, who was both a director and a shareholder, then petitioned the court to have the company wound up on the "just and equitable" ground, and, in case that failed, petitioned also, on the grounds of unfair prejudice, for the money to be returned (which was done) and for a forensic audit of the company's books to be carried out at the respondent's expense. The court granted the winding-up order on the ground that the way the company had been run had destroyed confidence.

Essential Facts

- Companies are legal persons and, therefore, where a wrong has been done to a company, the company is the proper pursuer. This is the rule in *Foss* v *Harbottle*, also known as the principle of majority rule.

- If the board of directors, or one or more of them, has committed a breach of duty in relation to the company, and neither the board of directors nor the members are prepared to raise an action against the wrongdoer in the name of the company, it may be possible for a minority member or members to petition the court for authority to do so, under rules in ss 265–269 of the Companies Act 2006 (statutory derivative action).

- The existence of the new statutory derivative action does not affect the fact that a minority member is allowed to raise a personal action to seek a personal remedy if he has suffered from breach of duty by the directors (s 265(6)(a)).

- It is open to a minority member to present a petition alleging that a company's affairs are being or have been or are going to be conducted in a manner that is unfairly prejudicial to the interests of members generally, or some part of the members, including at least himself (ss 994–999 of the Companies Act 2006). Various remedies can be sought under these sections, but the most frequently sought is an order to have the company or another shareholder buy the petitioner's shares from him.

- As a last resort, it is possible to petition the court for an order to have the company wound up on the ground that it is just and equitable to do so (s 122(1)(g) of the Insolvency Act 1986). There are restrictions in these rules to ensure that they are only used as a last resort where all trust between the parties has broken down and where it is not possible to use some other remedy such as a petition alleging unfairly prejudicial conduct.

Essential Cases

Foss v Harbottle (1843): this case articulates the principle of majority rule, which usually prevents a minority member of a company from raising an action seeking a remedy for a company for a wrong allegedly done to it, if the company as a legal person could do so itself.

Wishart, Petitioner (2010): provided the two tests in s 268(1) of the Companies Act 2006 are satisfied, namely (i) that the directors of a company who are complying with their duties would not have refused to raise the proceedings and (ii) that the act or omission complained of has not been authorised or ratified, and the court has taken into account other matters in s 268(2) designed to sift out unmeritorious cases, the court can grant leave to bring the derivative action. Also, the courts in Scotland can grant an order authorising the petitioner to be indemnified for his expenses in bringing the derivative action by the company.

Pender v Lushington (1877): a member who has suffered personally from a breach of duty at the hands of the directors of a company can bring proceedings seeking a personal remedy.

Robertson, Petitioner (No 1) (2009): in an unfair prejudice case, where the court has ordered the petitioner to buy out the shares of the respondent, rather than the other way round, the court could approve a deduction of losses from the respondent's shares, to reflect losses from trading in a foreign exchange which had been carried on without the knowledge or approval of the petitioner.

West Coast Capital (LIOS) Ltd, Petitioners (2008): in the course of an unfair prejudice petition, an interim interdict to prevent a resolution for the allotment of further shares being put to a general meeting was refused because of insufficient evidence of its potential impact on the parties and the company.

Re Saul Harrison & Sons plc (1995): where there was no underlying informal relationship between the parties, making it unfair for the company to be run in accordance with the Articles of Association, in order for an unfair prejudice petition to succeed, it would have to be proved that the Articles had been infringed or that members of management had used their powers for an improper purpose, neither of which were established in this case.

Re Bovey Hotel Ventures Ltd (1981): in order to establish unfairly prejudicial conduct, the petitioner did not have to show that the persons controlling the company knew they were acting unfairly or in bad faith. The test was whether a reasonable bystander, observing the consequences of the conduct, would regard it as having unfairly prejudiced the petitioner's interests.

Re London School of Electronics Ltd (1986): although it was not a requirement for bringing a petition on the ground of unfairly prejudicial conduct that the petitioner's conduct be above reproach, the fact that the petitioner's conduct might itself be prejudicial towards the company might affect the relief the court was prepared to grant.

Re Astec (BSR) plc (1998): in a listed public company, parties must expect that it will be run strictly in accordance with its Articles of Association, and, if there was no breach of directors' duties, there was no scope to claim that legitimate expectations had been ignored, and no grounds for an unfair prejudice petition.

O'Neill v Phillips (1999): ordinarily, to succeed in a petition alleging unfairly prejudicial conduct, breach of the rules on which the petitioner had agreed the company had been conducted or use of the rules in a manner that contravenes good faith would need to be proved. The case set out guidance on the concept of unfairness, in an effort to introduce some legal certainty and restrict the growth of the concept of legitimate expectations by shareholders in relation to their companies. The case also makes clear that the statutory provisions on unfairly prejudicial conduct are not to be used as a form of "no fault divorce".

Re D & R Chemicals Ltd (1989): dilution of a minority's shareholding so that it could no longer defeat a special resolution could be unfairly prejudicial conduct.

Johnson v Gore Wood (No 1) (2002): where a company has been successful in claiming damages, a shareholder will not be able to raise proceedings personally if his losses are merely reflective of the company's own losses.

Weir v Rees (1991): the courts in Scotland have power to appoint a judicial factor to act as an interim manager to protect the company's affairs.

Jesner v Jarrad Properties Ltd (1994): where trust and confidence in the management of a family company has been lost, it may be appropriate for the company to be wound up on the just and equitable ground in s 122(1)(g) of the Insolvency Act 1986.

12 CAPITAL MAINTENANCE

In Chapter 10 the rules of allotment of shares by companies were discussed. This chapter looks further at the share capital of companies and the restrictions on what companies are allowed to do with their share capital. Companies may wish to reduce their share capital if their business needs change, or they may wish to acquire their own shares or assist others to do so by providing financial assistance. When they have made a profit, many companies wish to pay a dividend. All of these activities are allowed, but have restrictions attached to them to protect their creditors, which will be explored in this chapter.

The basic principle behind the restrictions springs from the fact that most companies are limited liability companies, and creditors can only look to the company for payment, and not, as in a partnership, also to the partners personally. There was an early rule in the case law that capital, once raised, must be maintained for the benefit of the creditors. This rule is often referred to as the "creditors' buffer". The position taken in the old case law was that, though companies might lose capital through poor trading and economic shocks, they could not deliberately set out to reduce their capital without a court order, even if a company's constitution might expressly provide for that. The House of Lords case of *Trevor* v *Whitworth* (1887) is a good example of that strict approach.

The modern rules have been influenced greatly by the European Union, which in the Second Company Law Directive (77/91/EEC) made rules for public companies in the European Union on the maintenance and alteration of capital. These have since been amended by a further Directive (2006/68/EC), and for the UK they are found in the Companies Act 2006 as modified by statutory instrument.

Generally, the restrictions apply most strictly to public companies, and particularly listed companies, with a greater amount of freedom for private companies.

REDUCTION OF CAPITAL

There are rules in the Companies Act 2006 to ensure that when a company raises capital, it receives either money or money's worth for that capital. The capital may be paid up at the time when the shares are issued, or it may be paid up later. At the very latest, it is paid up at the time of the liquidation of the company. Although some companies do not have a significant share capital, and may perhaps only issue two £1 shares as a notional issued share capital, other companies do rely on their share capital to finance their activities, and this is particularly true of listed public companies. For this reason, there are restrictions on the reduction of capital by companies.

A company might wish to reduce capital for a range of reasons. It might be that it no longer has a need for such a large capital. Or there may be a class of shares with unattractive rights attached, which the company wishes to dispense with. Or in a private company, the company might buy a member's shares and may use capital to do so, as will be discussed later in this chapter. Depending on the circumstances, a reduction of capital may or may not result in capital being returned to members, as it may be that the reduction simply removes their obligation to take shares in future, or cancels paid-up capital that is lost or is not represented by assets. One limitation applying to all companies is that a reduction of capital must not leave the company with nothing except redeemable shares, because the company could then commit a kind of "suicide" by redeeming all its shares as they would then be cancelled, as will be shown later in this chapter. Also, if the reduction of capital of a public company would reduce the capital below the threshold of £50,000, the company would have to re-register as a private company.

The rules of reduction of capital are in ss 641–653 of the Companies Act 2006. Under these rules a private company may reduce capital if it passes a special resolution to do so, supported by a declaration of solvency by the directors. The declaration of solvency is to the effect that there are no grounds for considering that the company is unable to pay its debts, and that if the company were intended to be wound up within 12 months, it would be able to pay its debts in full within a further 12 months from the commencement of the winding up, and in other cases that it will be able to pay its debts as they fall due within the year following the reduction of capital. Making a declaration of solvency without having reasonable grounds for believing the opinion expressed in it to be true, is an offence on the part of the directors. A copy of the special resolution and the declaration of solvency have to be registered at Companies House along with a statement showing the company's capital after the reduction within 15 days of the passing of the resolution, at which point the resolution for the reduction of capital takes effect.

In the case of a public company, not only does this procedure of passing a special resolution and granting a declaration of solvency apply, but there must also be an application to the court. A private company is also at liberty to use this procedure if it wishes. If the reduction of capital involves a reduction in liability in respect of unpaid share capital or a repayment to a shareholder of any paid-up capital, then any creditor has the right to object to the court. However, to have a valid objection, creditors must be able to show that their claim is potentially at risk and that the company has not taken sufficient safeguards. Before the court can confirm the reduction, it must be satisfied that every creditor has either consented, or the debt has been discharged, or secured (s 648). The court order is then registered at Companies House with the statement of capital, which is the point at which it takes effect.

ACQUISITION BY A COMPANY OF ITS OWN SHARES

Until 1981 it used to be forbidden in the UK for a company to acquire its own shares, even if the constitution of a company so provided, as in *Trevor* v *Whitworth* (1887). The major reason for this was to ensure that a company could not create a false market in its own shares. The starting position for the current rules in the Companies Act 2006 is still that of a prohibition, backed by criminal penalties applying to the company and its officers, but one that allows of some exceptions. The modern rules implement the Second Company Law Directive (as amended), which affects public companies, and consequently stricter rules apply to them than to private companies.

Section 658 states: "A limited company may not acquire its own shares, whether by purchase, subscription, or otherwise, except in accordance with this part."

A company is allowed to acquire its own shares in the following circumstances and where various safeguards are met:

- in a reduction of capital, described above;
- the purchase of shares by a company made in fulfilment of a court order, eg where a court orders the company to purchase shares of a minority member who has suffered unfair prejudice as described in Chapter 11;
- where shares are forfeited to a company for non-payment of a call on shareholders to pay up their shares;
- the issue of redeemable shares and their redemption, discussed further in this chapter;
- the purchase by a company of its own shares, discussed further in this chapter;
- gifts to a company of its own shares.

When a company acquires its own shares, the shares must usually be cancelled on acquisition. However, a listed company or public company with its shares traded on the London Stock Exchange or the Alternative Investment Market or another regulated market is allowed to hold its own shares until it can resell them (treasury shares) under ss 724–732, provided that the shares were purchased out of distributable profits (see below), no voting rights are exercised on them, and no dividend is paid or bonus shares issued in respect of them. Treasury shares may be either sold for cash or transferred to an employees' share scheme.

Redemption and purchase by a company of its own shares

Redeemable shares are shares which are stated in the terms of issue to be redeemable either at some specific time in the future, or if some event occurs. They might be used to enable a venture capitalist to take an equity stake in a company, and still have the comfort of having an exit route from a company where there may be no market in its shares. Subject to safeguards for the protection of creditors, companies are allowed to redeem such shares and may also purchase their own shares, even shares which are not stated to be redeemable.

If a public company is to be able to issue redeemable shares, it must have power to do so in its Articles, whereas a private company will usually have that power unless the Articles restrict it (s 684). A purchase by a company of its own shares must be authorised by the Articles (s 690). If a company is to have power to redeem any shares, there must be other shares in issue which are not redeemable (s 684). Redemption can take place only if the shares are fully paid (s 686), which is also the case for purchase by a company of its own shares (s 691).

Funding for the redemption or purchase by a company of its own shares

In both redemption and purchase by a company of its own shares, the company must usually pay for the shares out of distributable profits (usually also including any premium on redemption or purchase) or out of the proceeds of a fresh issue of shares made for the purpose. A private company is, however, allowed to make limited use of capital, as discussed below.

The shares that are redeemed or purchased are cancelled, so the amount of the issued share capital is diminished accordingly. As a result of this, unless the redemption or purchase is financed by the proceeds of a fresh issue of shares made for the purpose, where the new share issue replaces the capital redeemed or purchased, in cases where the funding comes from distributable profits, steps have to be taken to fill the void. This is done by the creation of a *capital redemption reserve*, if any part of the funding comes from distributable profits. In such a case, an amount equal to the amount by which the share capital is diminished must be credited to a capital redemption reserve, which is treated as a capital account (s 733). By this means, except where capital is used to fund the redemption or purchase by a private company, capital is maintained.

A private company has a limited power to use capital to fund the redemption or purchase of its own shares. If it does so, then capital will be reduced at the end of the exercise. In some circumstances, a company might wish to use this power: for example, to end a relationship with an obstructive shareholder, or in a family business to finance the purchase of shares from a shareholder who wishes to retire. The purchase by a private company of its shares using capital is possible under rules in ss 709–723. These provide that distributable profits must first be exhausted before capital can be used. The shortfall between the amount of distributable profits or of the proceeds of any fresh issue of shares and the sum needed to redeem or purchase the shares is the "permissible capital payment". The company must authorise the payment out of capital by passing a special resolution, on which the member whose shares are to be purchased using capital is not allowed to vote.

There are various rules designed to ensure that a payment out of capital does not fatally weaken the company so that it cannot pay its debts and the creditors suffer. The directors must make a declaration of solvency under s 714 to the effect that they are of the opinion that the company is solvent and will be able to carry on business and pay its debts in full over the coming year, taking into account all the company's liabilities. This declaration of solvency has to be backed by an auditor's report confirming that the permissible capital payment has been properly determined and that he is not aware of any circumstances which would suggest that the directors' declaration of solvency is unreasonable in the circumstances. The company must advertise the proposed payment in the *Edinburgh Gazette* and in a national newspaper circulating in the part of the UK where the company is registered, and make the directors' statement and auditors' report available for inspection for 5 weeks from the date of the resolution. These documents can be inspected by any member or creditor without charge. During the 5-week period, any member or creditor of the company may apply to the court for the cancellation of the resolution. The payment out of capital cannot be made until the end of 5 weeks and must be made before the end of 7 weeks from the date of the resolution.

The court has the power to order the purchase of shares of dissentient members and to order arrangements to be made for the protection of dissentient creditors (such as the provision of security for their claims) and the court must make an order either cancelling or confirming the resolution for redemption or purchase of shares out of capital. The order may extend the date for the payment to be made and may make consequential changes to the Articles of Association, or may prohibit the company from making changes to the Articles of Association without the leave of the court. Notice of application to court and the court order itself must be registered at Companies House.

A company can either purchase its own shares privately by contract with a shareholder or shareholders (off-market purchase), or a listed public company could make a market purchase and buy its shares through the London Stock Exchange, the Alternative Investment Market or some other market. A company might wish to make a market purchase if it has surplus distributable profit, the aim being to increase the value of the remaining shares.

Market purchase

A market purchase must be authorised by an ordinary resolution under s 701. This must set out the maximum number of shares to be acquired and the maximum and minimum prices that are authorised to be paid. This is because prices on the Stock Exchange and other markets fluctuate all the time and it would be impossible to know whether any price set in advance would be one at which a deal could be struck. The authority must state its expiry date, which can be up to 5 years after the date of the resolution.

Off-market purchase

In an off-market purchase there must first be a special resolution to authorise a contract to be made for the purchase of the shares at a particular price (s 694). A copy of the contract or, if the contract is unwritten, a memorandum setting out its terms must be available for inspection for 10 years from the date of the resolution either at the company's registered office or at another office notified to Companies House. These may be inspected free of charge by members and in a public company by any other person, on pain of criminal penalties on the company and its officers in case of default.

A considerable amount of disclosure has to be made when a company redeems or purchases its own shares. A return has to be made to Companies House following the redemption or purchase giving details of the new share capital (s 689 for redemption and s 707 for purchase). Where shares are cancelled on purchase by the company (which is usually the case unless a listed public company holds them as treasury shares, as explained above), notice of cancellation must be given to Companies House with a statement of capital. Also, the fact that the company has redeemed or purchased its own shares must be disclosed in the next set of Annual Accounts.

When companies redeem or purchase their own shares, they should perform the contract right away (ss 686 and 691). If, despite contracting to redeem or purchase its own shares, the company does not honour that contract at the time, the normal remedies that would usually be available in cases of breach of contract are somewhat modified. By s 735, it is not possible for the affected shareholder or shareholders to claim damages. Also, if the company can show that it cannot meet the payment out of distributable profits, the same section provides that specific performance (specific implement in Scotland) cannot be used either. The reason for these restrictions is to ensure that the company is not put into the position that it is forced to make a payment out of capital. If the company goes into insolvent liquidation before the shares have been redeemed or purchased, the unpaid shareholder will be a postponed creditor.

FINANCIAL ASSISTANCE BY A COMPANY FOR THE PURCHASE OF ITS SHARES

Like the purchase by a company of its own shares, until the early 1980s it used to be prohibited for a company to provide financial assistance to enable people to buy shares in the company. The reasons for the prohibition were similar to the reasons for the prohibition of purchase by a company of its own shares: financial assistance could be used to manipulate the share price and enable a false market in the shares of listed companies to be created; it might allow acquisitions of companies by asset-strippers which would, on acquisition of the company, then cherry-pick some parts of the company for retention and sell off the rest, with consequent loss of jobs.

Financial assistance for the purchase of shares might, for example, take the form of a loan, a guarantee by the company, or the use of the company's assets as security for borrowing by the purchaser, a gift by the company to the purchaser to help with the purchase of shares, or the discharge by the company of a liability incurred by the purchaser.

Since the early 1980s, certain kinds of financial assistance can legally be provided by a company, the current rules being found in ss 677–683 of the Companies Act 2006. Changes were made in the Companies Act 2006 whereby private companies may freely give financial assistance unrestricted by these rules, except where a private company is the holding company of a public company, when the following rules apply, as they do to public companies.

For public companies, there is a prohibition backed by criminal penalties on the giving of financial assistance by a public company or its subsidiary for the acquisition of shares in a public company before or at the same time as the acquisition takes place (s 678). There is also a prohibition on a public company giving financial assistance after the acquisition of the company has taken place, provided that the company is still a public company at that point. If the company re-registers as a private company between the time of the acquisition and the time the financial assistance is given, the arrangement will be legal.

However, these prohibitions contain exceptions. Under ss 678 and 679, financial assistance will be lawful if the principal purpose in giving the assistance is not the giving of financial assistance itself, or the assistance is part of a larger purpose and the assistance is given in good faith in the interests of the company. The idea behind this test is to permit the kind of arrangement like an employee buy-out, where the company's assets are used as security for the employees' borrowings, and where the buy-out is designed to continue to run a profitable venture for the benefit of all concerned, while prohibiting the asset-stripper where the purchase is not motivated by good faith and the interests of the company are not the main concern. However, the words of these subsections are very general and have given rise to litigation, notably in the case of *Brady* v *Brady* (1989). That case concerned private companies, which at the time were subject to these rules, but with some more flexibility than was the case for public companies, although that fact appeared not to have been noticed until the case reached the House of Lords.

There are various other statutory exemptions as well, where transactions that might otherwise be thought to be financial assistance for the purchase of a company's shares will not be considered to be unlawful. Some of these transactions listed in s 681 are there for the sake of clarity, because past court decisions had suggested that they might constitute financial assistance. They include payment of dividends, bonus shares, reduction of capital, redemption and purchase of a company's own shares. The rationale must be to make clear that the proceeds of these transactions might be recycled into the purchase of more shares in the company. Another exception relates to the lending of money in the ordinary course of a company's business and contributions to an employees' share scheme, but a public company can only do this if it has net assets which are not reduced by the transaction, or, if they are reduced, if the finance comes from distributable profits.

If a company gives unlawful financial assistance, there are criminal consequences for the company itself and its officers under s 680. The Act does not spell out what the civil consequences are for the financial assistance contract. However, the House of Lords in *Brady* v *Brady* considered that the contract would be unenforceable because of the illegality. Other case law suggests that the illegality may also affect related transactions, if they are considered to be part of a single transaction, but not if they can be separated. Directors who advocate a transaction that is later viewed as an illegal financial assistance transaction might find themselves in breach of their directors' duties, since they have arguably caused the company to undertake a contract that is both illegal and probably not in the best interests of the company.

The rules on financial assistance by a company for the purchase of its shares are very imprecise and therefore dangerous to use, for fear of ending up embroiled in an illegal transaction with criminal penalties and problems with enforcement of contracts. The exceptions are difficult to use because it is impossible to know whether a court might take a different view of a transaction which the parties might view as being aimed at the good of the company. Detailed legal advice would be essential.

DIVIDENDS

A dividend is a distribution or share of profits that may be paid by a company to its shareholders. A company will have rules for the payment of dividends, which will usually be found in the Articles of Association.

The capital maintenance rules apply in their full rigour to the payment of a dividend. There are rules in the Companies Act 2006 on the funds out of which dividends may be paid. These rules reinforce an absolute prohibition on the payment of dividends out of capital. They can only be paid out of distributable profits, which is a stricter rule than that applying to the redemption or purchase by a company of its own shares. All companies have to satisfy one test and public companies must satisfy a second one before they can pay a dividend. The first test can be called the "realised profits" test, which relates to the profit and loss account: distributable profits are calculated as accumulated realised profits less accumulated realised losses (s 830). The word "accumulated" means that past losses cannot be written off, which might otherwise allow a company that has had a good year after a series of bad years, to pay a dividend despite an underlying bad financial position. The word "realised" is not defined in the statute but has been left to be determined by accounting practice; the general thrust is that revaluations of assets in the accounts cannot form the basis of paying a dividend, whereas the proceeds of a sale can.

Public companies have to undergo a second test: a "net assets" test. This is a balance sheet test by which public companies may not pay a dividend if their net assets (assets less liabilities) are less than the aggregate of their called-up share capital and undistributable reserves (s 831). The undistributable reserves include (i) the share premium account, which is created when shares are issued at a premium (more than their nominal value) (see Chapter 10), (ii) the capital redemption reserve (created if shares are redeemed or purchased using distributable profits, as discussed earlier in this chapter), (iii) the amount by which accumulated realised profits not previously utilised by capitalisation, which will be discussed later in this chapter, exceed accumulated realised losses not previously written off in a reduction or reorganisation of capital, and (iv) any other fund which is undistributable under statute or the articles of the company. The public company must continue to satisfy this test after the distribution.

Dividends are paid with reference to financial accounts (s 836). Companies often pay both a final dividend once the annual accounts are completed and an interim dividend half way through the year, if it appears that the company has made sufficient distributable profit to support a dividend. If a company wishes to pay an interim dividend, interim accounts may need to be drawn up if the most recent accounts would not support the payment of a dividend. If a company wishes to pay a dividend during its first year of trading, initial accounts would need to be drawn up. The accounts would usually be audited, except in those small companies which are audit exempt.

The Articles of Association will usually set out the rules for the payment of a dividend, and the Model Articles for both public and private companies do so: for example reg 70 of the Model Articles for public companies and reg 30 for private companies. These Articles empower the directors to recommend a dividend and for the members formally to declare the dividend by ordinary resolution. The members are not allowed to declare a larger dividend than the directors have recommended. These regulations allow the directors to determine how much of the distributable profit needs to be retained to fund the company's operations over the coming year and longer, and how much should be used to fund the dividend. The dividend is then paid according to the rights of the various classes of shareholders that the company may have, with any preference shareholders usually receiving their fixed dividends before the equity shareholders.

Dividends may be payable in cash or in kind, ie assets, if the Articles permit, although they are usually paid in cash. Sometimes dividends are paid in the form of further shares in the company if the Articles permit.

A dividend only becomes a debt due to a member once it has been formally declared. This means that shares are inherently more risky investments than loans to companies: with a loan, the company incurs a debt to the lender from the outset, and the obligation to repay will usually also incur interest.

If a company breaches the rules and pays a dividend out of capital, that payment is an unlawful distribution under s 847. That section provides that if a member receives an unlawful distribution knowing or having reasonable grounds to believe that it has been paid in breach of the rules, the recipient is liable to repay it to the company. However, the section does not affect other legal consequences that may apply.

In *Precision Dippings Ltd* v *Precision Dippings Marketing Ltd* (1986) Precision Dippings paid a dividend to its parent company Precision Dippings Marketing Ltd at a time when the members knew that the auditors' report was qualified, but did not know how material the qualification was at that time. Precision Dippings later went into liquidation. The liquidator sought the repayment of the dividend as an unlawful distribution. The court held that it had to be repaid because it was not open to the members to ignore the qualification in the auditors' report by voting to do so, as it was not just a procedural irregularity, even though it was eventually revealed by the auditors that the qualification was not material. The dividend had therefore to be returned to the liquidator.

A hard line was taken by the court in *It's a Wrap (UK) Ltd* v *Gula* (2006). Here the company's accountant had advised the directors and shareholders of a small company that the most tax efficient way to pay them for their work was for them to receive dividends rather than draw salaries. However, that advice presupposed that the company continued to make distributable profits. The company paid them a dividend when it had no profit. The court held that they were liable to repay the dividends, even though they had not known that the payment was illegal. As they did know that the company had no profits, the court took the line that ignorance of the law is no excuse, and forced them to repay.

The directors may also not escape liability, as they may be found to have breached their statutory directors' duties. A very old case, *Flitcroft's Case* (1882), established the principle that a director who pays dividends out of capital will be liable to compensate the company. The case is also authority for the fact that the members, even if they had known the true facts, cannot ratify an improper payment of dividends so as to bind the company. *Bairstow* v *Queen's Moat Houses plc* (2001) is a more modern authority for the fact that directors may be liable to compensate the company for an unlawful distribution. The case took place when directors' duties were still found in the common law, but the position would be unlikely to be different today, as the requirements for directors signing off the accounts are now even more onerous. In that case, the directors were aware that dividends had been paid on accounts that did not show a true and fair view. The directors were held liable to repay the amount of the dividend, and liability did not depend on whether or not the company was solvent at the time. The Court of Appeal held that the directors would not escape liability by being able to claim that they acted honestly and reasonably and should be excused under what is now s 1157, as they had acted dishonestly in this case, although that might be possible to plead in different circumstances.

BONUS SHARES

Bonus shares are also called scrip issues and capitalisation issues. If a company has a large amount of retained profit that it is unable to use in trading, it may be that the company's net asset value exceeds the value of its legal capital. The company may wish to increase the legal capital by using that surplus distributable profit to fund the issue of additional shares to its existing shareholders. A company is allowed to fund the purchase of these shares not only out of distributable profits, but also out of a share premium account, if it has one, by virtue of s 610. The effect of the issue of bonus shares is likely to be to dilute the value of the existing issued shares.

SERIOUS LOSS OF CAPITAL

The Second Company Law Directive places an obligation on the directors of a public company which suffers a "serious loss of capital" to convene an extraordinary general meeting to discuss what to do about the issue. A serious loss of capital under s 656 arises where the net assets of the company have fallen to half or less of its called-up share capital. There is a timetable for the meeting to take place, according to which they have 28 days to convene the meeting from the date on which they first became aware of the issue, and the extraordinary general meeting must take place within 56 days from that date. Default is a criminal offence. The section does not oblige the company to do anything at all but, depending on the circumstances, things that might be considered would include in extreme cases putting the company into administration or liquidation, refinancing the company by additional borrowing, or a reorganisation of the company or a group of companies, as will be discussed in Chapter 16.

POSSIBLE REFORM OF THE SECOND COMPANY LAW DIRECTIVE

As has already been mentioned in this chapter, parts of the Second Company Law Directive were amended in 2006. A High Level Group of Company Law Experts was appointed by the European Commission to consider the provision of a Modern Regulatory Framework for Company Law in Europe, and made its final report in 2002. It considered the concept and function of legal capital in some depth and explored alternative means of creditor protection, other than by the capital maintenance rules of the Second Company Law Directive. It considered that the most important issue for creditors was the ability of the company to pay its debts in the short and long term rather than maintenance of its legal capital, which does not always well reflect the ability of a company to pay its debts. The Group also considered the argument that capital maintenance might be an unduly inflexible restraint on companies. The report identified various amendments that could be made to the Directive, which were later made in 2006, some of which have been discussed in this chapter. It was suggested that further research should be done into identifying an alternative and optional system by which the concept of legal capital could be abolished, but shareholder control over decisions that affect shareholders' equity could be retained. It was considered that such a system might be based on a declaration of solvency, to be made before any reduction of capital or payment of a revenue distribution might be made. In the case of a dividend payment, both a net assets test and a test of the company's continued ability to pay its debts as they fall due over the coming year might be used. A feasibility study was commissioned from the accountancy firm KPMG, which reported in 2008. The findings after consultation were that the existing rules on legal capital did not hamper the distribution of dividends, and that the Second Directive did not restrict Member States from imposing an additional solvency test if thought fit. For these reasons, the European Commission is not intending to pursue further changes to the Second Company Law Directive in the immediate future.

Essential Facts

- There is a rule that stems from the case law and is now found in statutory form, enacting European Union rules in the Second Company Law Directive, that capital once raised must be maintained intact for the benefit of the creditors and cannot be returned to the members, except where safeguards for the protection of the creditors allow.

- A reduction of capital will reduce the company's legal capital, so that capital will not be maintained. It may result in capital being returned to members, but not in every case. Safeguards are needed in both private and public companies. In all companies there must be a special resolution by the shareholders and a declaration of solvency by the directors. In addition, a public company must obtain the approval of the court. These procedures are found in ss 641–653 of the Companies Act 2006.

- There is a general prohibition on the acquisition by a company of its own shares under s 658 of the Companies Act 2006. The prohibition admits of various exceptions which include redemption and purchase by a company of its own shares, provided that statutory procedure is followed, and because the shares are usually cancelled, the capital is nevertheless maintained by the creation of a capital redemption reserve, if distributable profits are used to fund the redemption or purchase. A private company has a limited right to use capital to fund a redemption or purchase, and in these circumstances capital will not be maintained, but a declaration of solvency must be given. These rules are found in ss 684–723 of the Companies Act 2006.

- There are restrictions on public companies giving financial assistance for the purchase of their shares, which also apply to private companies that are the holding companies of public companies. These rules again take the form of a prohibition backed by criminal penalties, with exceptions. These rules are found in ss 677–683 of the Companies Act 2006.

- The rule of capital maintenance applies very strictly to the payment of dividends, which can only be paid out of distributable profits, and never out of capital. All companies are subject to a "realised profits" test before paying dividends. Public companies must also pass a "net assets" test before and after paying the dividend. If a dividend is paid out of capital illegally, it is an unlawful distribution and if the shareholders know or ought to know that it was paid from capital, they may have to repay it. The directors may also be liable for compensation for breach of duty. The statutory rules on payment of a dividend are found in ss 829–853 of the Companies Act 2006.

- Companies may decide to issue bonus shares (a capitalisation issue) by converting unused distributable profit into fully paid bonus shares. The share premium account can also be used for this, if the company has one.

- If a public company has suffered a "serious loss of capital" as defined in s 656, the directors must convene an extraordinary general meeting to decide what, if anything, needs to be done.

- The Second Company Law Directive has been amended to relax some of the rules. Further reform of this Directive has been proposed, to provide an alternative optional system to that of legal capital, whereby existing capital maintenance restrictions could be replaced by a solvency test. However, the European Commission does not consider that this is worth pursuing at this point.

Essential Cases

Trevor v Whitworth (1887): the company had Articles of Association which allowed it to purchase its own shares. The company had purchased the shares of a shareholder, but they had not been fully paid for by the time the company went into liquidation. The unpaid shareholder made a claim in the liquidation. The House of Lords held that as there was no power in the Companies Acts to allow a company to purchase its own shares, the claim must fail, despite the provision in the Articles.

Brady v Brady (1989): in an effort to allow warring factions in a family business to part ways, it was proposed that two businesses which had been run together be split as equally as possible. To make them equal, it was proposed that there be a transfer of assets in exchange for shares and this ended up in court as being unlawful financial assistance for the purchase of shares. The case is important for its discussion of the exceptions where financial assistance is part of a larger purpose and is given in good faith in the interests of the company. The House of Lords held that the transaction was in good faith but was not part of a larger purpose. However, the legality of the transaction was saved by a fact that appeared not to have been noticed in the lower courts, that as this was a private company, there were relaxations that applied at that time to private companies that would make the contract legal. Since the Companies Act 2006, private companies are now allowed to provide financial assistance for the purchase of their shares.

Precision Dippings Ltd v Precision Dippings Marketing Ltd (1986): if a dividend is paid according to accounts on which the members knew there was a qualified auditors' report, they could not approve the payment in these circumstances by a vote and would be liable to repay the dividend.

It's a Wrap (UK) Ltd v Gula (2006): where shareholders accepted dividends when they knew that the company had not made a profit, they were liable to repay the dividends even though they did not know the payment was illegal. The principle that ignorance of the law is no excuse applied.

Flitcroft's Case (1882): directors who allow dividends to be paid out of capital will be liable to compensate the company.

Bairstow v Queen's Moat Houses plc (2001): where directors were aware that accounts which did not show a true and fair view were used to support the payment of a dividend, the directors were liable to compensate the company, and, where they had acted dishonestly, they would not be able to rely on what is now s 1157, to excuse directors from liability if they have acted honestly and reasonably.

13 CREDITORS

There has been a great deal of discussion in Chapters 10 and 12 about the position of the shareholders of the company. Chapter 12 introduced the concept of creditor protection, which is inherent in the principle of maintenance of capital. In this chapter the position of the creditors of the company will be further explored. To put things in perspective, it is worth bearing in mind that a considerable number of companies have virtually no share capital at all, and exist with a token issued share capital of £2. However, almost every company will need to borrow money from time to time to finance its trading activities, making this a very important issue for companies.

UNSECURED AND SECURED CREDITORS

A person (perhaps a bank) may lend money to a company under a contract which demands that the money be repaid at some time in future, and usually that interest is paid on the loan. The loan may be open-ended, or it may have a fixed term. If the loan is not secured over assets belonging to the debtor, the remedies of the creditor are restricted to raising a civil action for debt or putting the debtor company into administration or liquidation. However, if the debt is secured over property belonging to the debtor company, the creditor has an additional remedy of being able to call up the loan and to enforce repayment out of the proceeds of sale of the property, with a higher priority for payment in relation to unsecured creditors.

If a debtor gives security for a loan, generally the lender will give better terms than for an unsecured loan, including a longer borrowing period, smaller repayments and a better rate of interest.

When a company borrows money, there are no restrictions as to the funds that may be used for repayment, in contrast to the payment of a dividend on share capital. The position is that the company has incurred a debt according to the terms of the contract, and repayments are due on that contract notwithstanding the fact that the company may have made no profits.

A listed public company may wish to issue debenture stock, which can be traded on the London Stock Exchange or any other market in a similar way to shares. Debenture stock will usually be secured. It can be traded in a similar way to shares.

FORMS OF SECURITY

In Scotland the law of property is different from the law in other parts of the United Kingdom. Consequently, different rules apply between Scotland and other parts of the United Kingdom as regards the forms of security that may be granted over the company's property. This chapter is concerned with only the rules that apply in Scotland. Even the terminology is different, as in Scotland the term "security" is usually used, whereas in England the term "charge" is preferred.

A security can be either *fixed or floating.*

Fixed charges or securities

A fixed security or charge is granted over specific and identifiable property. While the security is in existence, the debtor can use the property but is not able to sell it without the lender's permission. If the debtor fails to pay the debt, the lender can ultimately take possession of the property and sell it to recover the amount of the debt. Once the loan has been repaid the property will be handed back to the company.

Different forms of fixed security can be granted over different forms of property. A security over land or buildings in Scotland (heritable property) must be in the form of a standard security under the Conveyancing and Feudal Reform (Scotland) Act 1970. The security is in written form as set out in the Act and must be executed formally by the company and registered in the Land Register in Edinburgh and also at Companies House, as will be discussed below. A standard security can only cover land and buildings, and cannot apply to other forms of property.

A security can also be taken over incorporeal moveable property belonging to the company. This type of property consists of rights. Examples include shares owned by the company, insurance policies taken out by the company, and intellectual property rights owned by the company such as patents. Rights in all of these can be passed to the lender for the duration of the loan by a written document called an assignation in security. In the case of a security over shares, the shares would be temporarily transferred to the lender for the duration of the loan by a stock transfer form as described in Chapter 10. Some of these types of security also have to be registered at Companies House. Registration at Companies House will be considered below.

If a company wanted to grant a security over corporeal moveable property such as vehicles, machinery, office furniture, or other valuable and durable physical assets, the method to use is the "pledge", also known as "pawn". The problem with the pledge is that the assets have to be handed over to the pledgee or pawnbroker for the duration of the loan and cannot be used by the company, making this form of security impractical for companies, unless they have physical assets they can spare. One exception relates to whisky while it is maturing in a bonded warehouse, as the whisky will not be needed for a number of years, and the documents of title can be delivered to the lender, constituting a type of pledge under the Factors Act 1889 as applied to Scotland by the Factors (Scotland) Act 1890.

Floating charges

A security can be granted on the basis that it will not be fixed to particular assets for the duration of the loan, but will "float" so that a company will be free to buy and sell assets in the course of trade. As this form of security was borrowed from English law, the English term "floating charge" is used. Floating charges were introduced to Scots law by statute in 1961 and are not the same as English floating charges, which have their origins in case law. The power to grant a floating charge in Scotland is still found in s 462 of the Companies Act 1985, although this will be replaced by a similar provision in s 38 of the Bankruptcy and Diligence etc (Scotland) Act 2007 when it comes into force.

A floating charge in Scotland can be created over all types of property, both heritable and moveable. The company is free to buy and sell its assets in the course of trade, and to grant further securities over the same assets. Assets can be sold without the permission of the lender. When assets are sold they automatically pass out of the charge, and when assets are bought they automatically become subject to the charge. The charge will, however, become fixed to the particular assets that are owned by the company at the time when certain events occur that will cause this to happen, either under statute or under the terms of issue of the charge. This process is often referred to as the "crystallisation" of the floating charge, though this is not a statutory term. A floating charge will become fixed if any of the following events occur:

- the appointment of a receiver by a floating charge creditor under s 53(7) and 54(6) of the Insolvency Act 1986 where this is still permitted (this will be discussed further in Chapter 14);

- the commencement of the winding up of the company – s 463 of the Companies Act 1985 (to be replaced by s 45 of the Bankruptcy and Diligence etc (Scotland) Act 2007 when it comes into force);
- the appointment of an administrator where the administrator files notice with Companies House under para 115 of Sch B1 to the Insolvency Act 1986.

A floating charge in Scotland has to be "created" by a written document by the company, which must be registered (as will be described below). By s 879 of the Companies Act 2006, the date of creation is the date of execution of the document by the company.

Registration of fixed and floating charges

With a few exceptions, fixed and floating charges have to be registered in various registers. The purpose of this is to provide up-to-date information to potential creditors of the extent of the existing secured borrowing of the company, in addition to the information that the annual accounts will provide.

Registration in the Land Register – standard securities

Under the Conveyancing and Feudal Reform (Scotland) Act 1970, standard securities over heritable property have first to be registered in the Land Register in Scotland, in order to give the lender real rights over the land, ie rights in the property. They are "created" at the date of registration in this register rather than the date they were granted by the borrowing company. Only rights over land or buildings in Scotland will be capable of being registered in this register.

Registration in the proposed Register of Floating Charges – Scottish floating charges

Section 37 of the Bankruptcy and Diligence etc (Scotland) Act 2007 creates a register of floating charges. In future every floating charge granted by companies in Scotland will have to be registered in this register. Floating charges will be "created" from the date of registration in this register, rather than, as now, from the date they are executed by the company. It will be competent, though not obligatory, for a company and its lender to register advance notice of the intention to grant a floating charge. In that case, the floating charge will be backdated to the date the advance notice was given. This register will be maintained by Registers of Scotland, the public body which maintains the Land Register. At the time of writing, these provisions have not yet come into force, and there is no indication of when this might be. The reason for this change is to make floating charges publicly known at the time they are created, which is not the case at present, as will be seen in the next section of this chapter. This uncertainty has caused problems, which are discussed in Chapter 14.

Registration of charges at Companies House

Certain securities granted by companies registered in Scotland have to be registered with the Registrar of Companies under ss 878–892 of the Companies Act 2006. These are:

- securities over land or interests in land;
- securities over certain incorporeal moveable property:
  - goodwill
  - intellectual property rights (patents etc)
  - book debts
  - uncalled capital and unpaid calls on shares;
- securities over ships and aircraft;
- floating charges.

This list does not include all forms of security, and has been interpreted by the courts not to include securities over shares, securities over insurance policies, pledges and liens (which are securities that arise by operation of law).

Under s 886, the charge must be registered within 21 days of the date of creation. Failure to do this renders the charge void against the liquidator or administrator or any creditor and the money will become immediately repayable under s 889. The effect of this is that the company has a 21-day grace period during which it can register the charge and preserve its priority. If it fails to do so, other creditors who register a charge will have priority over this charge. Also, if the company were to go into administration or liquidation while the charge is unregistered, the creditor will be unable to obtain any security at all. Late registration is possible only in exceptional circumstances where the court allows it under s 888. Failure to register a charge within the prescribed time period is also a criminal offence on the part of the company and its officers under s 878.

When a charge is properly registered, the Registrar grants a certificate of the registration of a charge, which is conclusive evidence that the registration requirements have been satisfied (s 885).

The reason for the proposal to create a Register of Floating Charges in Scotland is because, during the 21-day grace period for registration, the current system gives rise to uncertainty as to whether or not there is a floating charge in place. In the new registration system, as and when it comes into force, the floating charge will take effect when it is registered in that register, and potential creditors have the opportunity to know of its existence from that date. This is discussed further in Chapter 14.

Registration in the company's own register of charges

A company must keep its own register of all fixed and floating charges either at its registered office or at another office notified to Companies House under ss 875–877. It must also make copies of all the written instruments creating the charges available for inspection. The register and the instruments must be available for inspection free of charge by all creditors and members of the company and by other persons on payment of a prescribed fee.

Priority of fixed and floating charges

As stated earlier in this chapter, under rules in the Companies Act 1985 which are still in force, floating charges in Scotland are created when the floating charge document is executed by the company. As explained, they must then be registered at Companies House within 21 days of the date of creation, but they do not become fixed to any particular assets unless and until they crystallise. This means that a fixed charge can be granted later than a floating charge and can obtain a higher ranking should the company become insolvent, because of the fact that the fixed security is fixed from the outset on particular assets. Section 464 of the Companies Act 1985 sets out the ranking of floating charges in relation to other claims:

- the document creating the floating charge may contain a prohibition on the creation of any later prior ranking or equally ranking fixed or floating charges; this is a negative pledge, and for Scottish companies this fact has to be registered at Companies House under s 885(3)(e);
- any fixed security arising by operation of law will have inherent priority over a floating charge;
- a fixed security which has established a real right over an asset before a floating charge has attached to the same asset has priority over a floating charge;

- floating charges rank against each other according to the date and time of registration and floating charges received for registration in the same post rank equally;

- where the holder of a floating charge receives written intimation of the registration of another floating charge over the same assets, the priority of the first floating charge over the subsequent one is restricted to security for the lender's present advances, future advances which the lender is contractually obliged to make under the instrument creating the charge, interest and expenses, after which the assets provide security for the lender on the second floating charge.

Once the new Register of Floating Charges comes into force for Scotland, this will change. From that time, floating charges will obtain their ranking position according to the date of their registration in that register.

Lenders often enter into ranking agreements to vary the ranking of claims that would usually apply in the event of the insolvency of the debtor company. The holder of a floating charge may also be able to prevent the creation of a later prior ranking security by a clause in the floating charge often referred to as a "negative pledge".

When a company that has granted a floating charge becomes insolvent, not every creditor will be paid in full. Usually, when that happens, each class of creditor is paid in turn and receives as much as there is available. Creditors in lower groups will not be paid if the money runs out when paying higher-ranking creditors. Floating charges generally rank more highly than ordinary creditors in relation to the assets that are subject to the security because they have a security over those assets, and, consequently, often very little or nothing is left after paying the floating charge creditor. The various insolvency regimes are discussed in Chapters 14 and 15. However, the Enterprise Act 2002 has made changes by which, for floating charges granted after the Enterprise Act 2002 came into force, provision has to be made for retention of money for the ordinary creditors when paying the floating charge creditor. A new s 176A of the Insolvency Act 1986 has been created which provides that when a company is in liquidation, administration, or receivership (where this is still allowed), a "prescribed part" must be kept back to pay the ordinary creditors. The amount of this is defined in a statutory instrument and is currently fixed at 50 per cent of the net property where the property subject to the floating charge is worth less than £10,000, and 50 per cent of the first £10,000 plus 20 per cent of the excess where the property subject to the charge is worth is more than £10,000, up to a limit of £600,000. This only applies to new floating charges granted after the date the provisions under the Enterprise Act 2002 came into force.

Proposals from the Department for Business, Innovation and Skills for amendments to the registration rules

A consultation paper was issued on 12 March 2010 on certain aspects of the current registration regime for charges in the UK. Responses were received and the Department reported in December 2010. Its view, in the light of the responses, is as follows:

- there should be a single UK-wide system for the registration of charges at Companies House which would apply to companies, limited liability partnerships, but not to overseas companies;
- all charges would have to be registered unless expressly excluded by legislation, to remove any remaining dubiety about the need for registration of certain charges; registration would be the responsibility of the person who takes the charge;
- the 21 days for registration of charges at Companies House should remain, but the criminal penalties for failure to register a charge in time should be removed; the civil consequences that apply at present will continue to apply;
- impediments to electronic filing of charge documents should be removed: currently companies have not been able to use electronic registration of title because of the need to file standard securities and floating charges in paper form at Companies House;
- in order to streamline registration procedures, the need to register a standard security more than once in different registers should be removed, so that by using powers of the Secretary of State in s 893 to allow information-sharing between registers, registration in the Land Register should enable sufficient information to be provided to Companies House; the same process would be followed for floating charges as and when the Register of Floating Charges comes into effect in Scotland;
- the certificate of registration from Companies House should continue to be conclusive evidence of the registration of the charge, but not of its extent;
- the need for the Registrar to maintain a register of charges should be abolished, as the copy of the charge is registered.

The Department for Business, Innovation and Skills is proposing to issue draft Regulations to implement these changes in 2011.

Essential Facts

- Most companies need to borrow money to support their business activities. Borrowing may be either unsecured or secured.

- With unsecured borrowing, the company is under a personal obligation to repay. If it defaults, it can be sued in a civil action or it can be put into administration or liquidation.

- With secured borrowing, the company has granted rights to a lender in security over some of its property. If the company defaults in its repayments, in additional to the remedies for unsecured borrowing, the lender can enforce rights over the property to obtain repayment of the sum owed.

- The forms of security that are available in Scotland are different from other parts of the United Kingdom because of differences in the law of property.

- Securities can be either fixed or floating.

- Most securities in Scotland have to be registered. Standard securities have to be registered in the Land Register. Most but not all securities including floating charges have to be registered, within 21 days of their date of creation, at Companies House. The company must also maintain its own register of charges.

- Currently there are rules for the ranking of floating charges against other floating charges in s 464 of the Companies Act 1985, which will change when the Register of Floating Charges comes into force – thereafter, floating charges will obtain their priority from their date of registration.

- By the Enterprise Act 2002, when a company that has granted a floating charge also has ordinary creditors, it has to retain a prescribed sum of money to pay to ordinary creditors, when it pays a floating charge creditor. This is to ensure that there are some funds left to pay these creditors.

14 CORPORATE INSOLVENCY: RESCUE AND RECEIVERSHIP

When an individual gets into financial difficulty and cannot pay his debts, the person can choose to become personally bankrupt, or his creditors may make him bankrupt (usually called sequestration in Scotland). Creditors are then paid in a certain ranking order, and, after a year in which the bankrupt's activities are restricted, the person is free to start again. For companies, *liquidation* (or winding up) provides a similar legal regime, the main difference being that the company does not start again, but will eventually be removed from the register of companies and cease to be a legal person.

If companies that could be saved are too hastily put into liquidation, there is a consequential economic loss for the country: employees lose their jobs, taxes are lost to the Exchequer, and products or services are no longer supplied, with exports lost to the country. Companies can therefore be put into *administration*, the main purpose being to try to rescue the company as a going concern if possible.

Where a company has granted a floating charge over its assets to secure its borrowing, as discussed in Chapter 13, the lender used to be able to put the company into *receivership* to enforce the security in priority to certain other creditors. However, this right is now greatly restricted as a result of changes brought in by the Enterprise Act 2002, following which floating charge creditors on new floating charges granted after the date of the change in the law are expected to use administration. The spur for the change was that too often receivership caused such harm to the prospects of the company that eventually it ended up beyond help and had to be put into liquidation.

This chapter is concerned with the legal regimes of receivership and administration. Some brief comments will also be made about *company voluntary arrangements*, another form of procedure aimed at rescuing struggling companies. The next chapter deals with liquidation (winding up).

The legislation is found in the Insolvency Act 1986, which has been substantially amended. The rules on administration apply to England and Wales and to Scotland, while the rules on liquidation are largely the same but with some variation for Scotland; and Scotland has its own rules on receivership because of the differences in the underlying law of property, mentioned in Chapter 13. Different rules apply to Northern Ireland.

In this chapter, whenever a section of a statute is mentioned without the name of the statute, it can be assumed that the reference is to a section of the Insolvency Act 1986.

THE PURPOSE BEHIND CORPORATE INSOLVENCY LAW

A system of corporate insolvency law should try to achieve the following:

- the preservation of those businesses that are capable of going on to prosper again;
- where a business cannot be saved, the rules should ensure that creditors are paid in an order that is seen by society to be fair;
- the public should be protected from abuse of the corporate form (and particularly of limited liability) by unscrupulous traders.

INSOLVENCY PRACTITIONERS

To make sure that the legal regimes for corporate insolvency are administered honestly, those who will be working as insolvency practitioners must hold qualifications under ss 388–398 of the Insolvency Act 1986. To be eligible, a person must be (i) an individual, (ii) not personally bankrupt or disqualified under the Company Directors Disqualification Act 1986 or suffering from mental incapacity, and (iii) a member of a recognised professional body such as the Institute of Chartered Accountants of Scotland, the ACCA, the Law Society of Scotland, or the Insolvency Practitioners Association, or authorised as a fit and proper person by the competent authority.

There are examinations that must be passed in order to practise as a qualified insolvency practitioner, in addition to the normal qualifications of the relevant professions.

No one can act as a qualified insolvency practitioner who (i) is personally bankrupt or subject to a bankruptcy restriction order, (ii) is subject to a disqualification order or disqualification undertaking under the Company Directors Disqualification Act 1986, or (iii) has a guardian appointed to him under the Adults with Incapacity (Scotland) Act 2000.

Acting as an insolvency practitioner without qualification is an offence.

An insolvency practitioner must also have no connections with the company.

All these rules are designed to keep the cowboys from working with insolvent companies, as otherwise there could be opportunities for the unscrupulous to do deals with the assets of the companies, which would not be in the interests of the creditors.

When an insolvency practitioner is appointed, they must find caution (pronounced "caytion", which is a kind of insurance under which the cautioner becomes jointly and severally liable) for their actions under s 390 of the Insolvency Act 1986 and the Insolvency Practitioners Regulations 2005 (SI 2005/524), covering the estate of the company from the consequences of the insolvency practitioner's fraud and dishonesty up to the level specified in the Regulations.

THE REGIMES OF CORPORATE INSOLVENCY LAW

Receivership

In Scotland, receivers can only be appointed where a company or a limited liability partnership has granted a floating charge to secure its borrowing. When floating charges were first brought into Scots law by statute in 1961, the law did not provide for receivers. However, eventually in 1972 a further statute provided for receivership in Scotland, and the current rules for Scotland are now found in ss 50–71 of the Insolvency Act 1986.

Receivership is more of an enforcement regime for a floating charge creditor than an insolvency regime. Although it was initially hoped that companies that went into receivership would emerge from it and trade again, experience proved too often that a company that went into receivership eventually ended up in liquidation. As a result of this, the Enterprise Act 2002 has now changed the rules for the future so that for companies with qualifying floating charges which were granted after 15 September 2003 (the date when these provisions of the Enterprise Act 2002 came into force), receivership will generally no longer be competent and instead administration has to be used – s 72A of the Insolvency Act 1986.

Receivership continues to be competent for floating charges granted prior to 15 September 2003, and also in certain exceptional cases, which include capital market arrangements of at least £50 million, lending related to companies involved in public–private partnerships, utility companies, urban regeneration projects and project finance where the finance provider is allowed to take over the contractor's role in the project (step-in rights), registered social landlords, and certain railway companies. As many companies prior to 2003 have granted floating charges to cover open-ended or long-term loans, these may run for many years to come, and consequently receivers will continue to be appointed for some time yet.

Appointment of a receiver

In cases where it is still competent to appoint a receiver, the instrument creating the floating charge will usually set out the circumstances in which this is competent. Often minimal notice is required. If nothing is specified, s 52 allows a receiver to be appointed by the holder of the floating charge in the following circumstances:

- if the floating charge creditor has made a demand for payment of the principal debt, and this has not been paid within 21 days;
- if interest payments have been in arrears for 2 months;
- if an order has been made by a court or a resolution passed by the company to put the company into liquidation;
- If the holder of another floating charge has appointed a receiver.

A receiver may also be appointed by the court on the application of the holder of the floating charge, although since the holder of the floating charge can do so without applying to court, use of this provision under s 52(2) of the Insolvency Act 1986 is unlikely. However, in order to have receivership recognised internationally where a company has cross-border assets, a court order would be needed. The court may appoint a receiver if any of the events listed in the first three points above are proved, or where the court is satisfied that the position of the holder of the floating charge is likely to be prejudiced if no such appointment is made.

If a receiver is appointed by the holder of a floating charge, it is done by a written instrument of appointment, of which a certified copy accompanied by notice of registration must be given to Companies House within 7 days of the date of execution under s 53 of the Insolvency Act 1986. Appointment by the court is done by petition to the court by the holder of the floating charge, after which a certified copy of the court's interlocutor appointing the receiver (court order) accompanied by notice of registration must be given to Companies House within 7 days of the grant of the interlocutor (s 54). Default is subject to criminal penalties.

When a receiver takes office, he must immediately inform the company of his appointment, and must inform all creditors within 28 days. His first task is to take stock of the company's financial position, and he must ask the directors to give him a statement of affairs showing the company's assets and liabilities and details of all creditors and the amounts of their claims and their securities. He will then decide what to do with the company, which may involve trying to find a buyer for the whole or part of the business. It may be that the company's financial position is too poor for there to be any chance of the survival of the business, and liquidation or even dissolution without liquidation may follow. In the course of a receivership, it is often necessary to make some employees redundant, which will be discussed later in this chapter.

Duties, powers and liability of the receiver

The reason why a floating charge creditor appoints a receiver is to safeguard the interests of the floating charge creditor. The business will probably still be running when the receiver takes office, and if the business is to be sold at a good price, or traded back to economic health, the receiver will keep the company trading. When a receiver takes office, the powers of the directors are suspended, and the receiver has powers to run the company similar to those the directors had. These powers are laid out in the document creating the floating charge; and there are additional powers in Sch 2 to the Insolvency Act 1986. However, if the floating charge relates to only some of the company's assets, the directors retain power to run the company in relation to the assets not subject to the charge. In a similar way to the exercise of a company's powers by the directors, third parties who deal with the receiver in good faith are entitled to assume that he is acting within his powers, by virtue of s 55(4) of the Insolvency Act 1986.

When a receiver contracts on behalf of the company, he does so as agent for the company with regard to the property subject to the floating charge, under s 57 of the Insolvency Act 1986, and he will be personally liable on these new contracts, unless he contracts out of that liability, which a receiver will usually do. This only applies to new contracts made by the receiver and does not affect existing contracts. The receiver has a right of indemnity for this personal liability out of the company's assets. By s 55, when a person contracts with the receiver in good faith and for value, he can rely on the receiver's having power to make a binding contract.

Although a receiver owes his principal duties to the floating charge creditor, he still owes duties to the company as he is the company's agent. In the English case of *Cuckmere Brick Co Ltd* v *Mutual Finance Ltd* (1971) a receiver was held to owe the company a duty of reasonable care to try to obtain a reasonable price in a sale of the company's property. The case law indicates that a receiver may have a duty to try to obtain the best price in a sale (*Standard Chartered Bank Ltd* v *Walker* (1982)) but not to have any obligation to postpone a sale in the hope of achieving a better price (*Tse Kwong Lam* v *Wong Chit Sen* (1983)). In the Scottish case of *Independent Pension Trustee Ltd* v *LAW Construction Co Ltd* (1997), the court held that if assets subject to a floating charge were under the control of a receiver, the directors could not exercise control of the same assets, as it would be impractical and contrary to principle to do so.

The position of the employees

When a receiver is appointed, the company is usually still trading, and the receiver has to decide whether it should continue to trade. One of his initial tasks will be to take stock of the workforce, and make decisions as to whether the company should continue to trade, and, if so, what size of workforce may be appropriate. The receiver has a grace period of the first 14 days in which to take these decisions. If the receiver adopts contracts of employment beyond that period, by asking the employees to continue to work for the company, the receiver is deemed to be the agent of the company with regard to contracts of employment adopted by him, by virtue of s 57(2). This means that the receiver assumes personal liability for payment of certain qualifying liabilities in respect of employees from the start of the receivership, unless they have contracted out of this. These include wages or salary, contributions to a pension scheme, holiday pay and sickness pay incurred since the receiver took office. Again, the receiver has a right of indemnity for this personal liability out of the company's assets.

Employees may be made redundant in the course of the receivership, and may have rights to a redundancy payment under the Employment Rights Act 1996 or, in cases of insolvent companies, to a claim on the National Insurance Fund for arrears of wages at £400 a week (from April 2011) for up to 8 weeks, holiday pay for up to 6 weeks at the same weekly rate, and pay in lieu of notice for a maximum of 12 weeks at the same weekly rate. A similar rule applies if a company is in administration or liquidation, both of which are covered later in this chapter. As will be seen below, an employee would have a claim as a preferential creditor as and when the company's assets are distributed.

The distribution of assets

The floating charge creditor is usually seeking the repayment of the floating charge in full. The receiver may have to sell assets or the whole or part of the business as a going concern. The floating charge creditor will rank with other creditors in a statutory order which is set out in ss 59 and 60 of the Insolvency Act 1986. The following creditors rank in the order stated below, in priority to the floating charge creditor:

- the holder of any *prior or equally ranking fixed security*;
- *any creditor who has effectually executed diligence* on any part of the property subject to the charge (these are creditors who have enforced court judgments over the property subject to the charge before the receiver is appointed);
- *creditors of the receiver* since taking office – it is important that these creditors have a high position in the ranking order, otherwise it would be impossible for the receiver to obtain the necessary credit on which to run the business;
- the *receiver* in respect of liabilities, expenses and remuneration and any indemnity he is entitled to out of the property of the company;
- *the preferential creditors* (these creditors are also given preference in the liquidation of the company). They are: unpaid contributions to occupational pension schemes and unpaid state pension scheme premiums for employees; unpaid salary or wages for a maximum of 4 months with a cap of £800 per employee, unpaid holiday pay, loans advanced to pay these wages or salary or holiday pay, and levies on coal and steel production. (The Government used to be a preferential creditor for unpaid PAYE income tax and VAT for 1 year and 6 months respectively, but these preferences were discontinued by the Enterprise Act 2002 and the Government is now an ordinary creditor.)

After all these debts have been paid in this order, the floating charge creditor can be paid. In a receivership, there is no provision for the payment of ordinary creditors. However, as explained earlier (in Chapter 13), the Enterprise Act 2002 has made changes following which, in relation to floating charges granted after that Act came into force, provision has to be made for retention of money for the ordinary creditors when paying the floating charge creditor. A new s 176A of the Insolvency Act 1986 has been created which provides that when a company is in liquidation, administration, or receivership (where this is still allowed), a "prescribed part" must be kept back to pay the ordinary creditors.

The amount of this is defined in a statutory instrument and is currently fixed at 50 per cent of the net property where the property subject to the floating charge is worth less than £10,000, and 50 per cent of the first £10,000 plus 20 per cent of the excess where the property subject to the charge is worth is more than £10,000, up to a limit of £600,000. This only applies to new floating charges granted after the date when these provisions under the Enterprise Act 2002 came into force.

Ordinary creditors of a company that has granted a floating charge may be able to protect their position in advance by including a provision in the contract for the sale of goods to the company to the effect that ownership of the goods is to be retained by the seller until the full price of the goods has been paid, or even until all balances on all contracts between the parties have been paid. This is very helpful when dealing with an insolvent company, as raw materials sold to the company with retention of title can then be reclaimed from the receiver and resold. Following the House of Lords' decision in *Armour* v *Thyssen Edelstahlwerke AG* (1990), complex retention of title clauses, which retain title over goods until balances on other contracts have been paid, have been held to be valid applications of rules in ss 17 and 19 of the Sale of Goods Act 1979.

The end of the receivership

Once the floating charge creditor has been paid, there may be another receiver under a later ranking floating charge who will take charge next. If the company is insolvent after paying the floating charge creditor, it will be put into liquidation. If the company is still solvent after paying the floating charge creditor in full, with no further floating charge creditors still to be paid, it could be handed back to its directors. It is also possible for a floating charge to refloat under s 62(6) if it is still in existence after the expiry of 1 month after the receiver has left office and no other receiver has taken office.

Problems with receivership

As noted at the start of the chapter, experience with receivership over the years was that too often receivership was eventually followed by the liquidation of the company. Also, it offered nothing to unsecured creditors. For these reasons, changes were made in the Enterprise Act 2002 with the aim of phasing out receivership for most companies, and replacing it by administration. Also, as mentioned above, for floating charges granted after 2003, some money has to be held back from payment of the floating charge creditors, to try to ensure that there is something to pay the unsecured creditors in a subsequent liquidation. This will be explored later in this chapter.

Another problem was revealed in the case of *Sharp* v *Thomson* (1997). The problem stemmed from the fact that a receiver might be appointed before a buyer could record the title to heritable property, and the fact of the appointment of the receiver might not be publicly known. In this case the Thomsons bought a flat from a company, paid the purchase price and took entry to the flat without having been granted a disposition which would given them legal title to the property once recorded. This transaction was very unusual, as usually a buyer does not pay the price and take entry until he has a disposition (deed) that can be recorded in the Land Register. The company had a floating charge over its assets, and the lender, in the usual way, gave the purchasers a certificate of non-crystallisation of the charge covering a time period, provided the disposition was recorded in 21 days, which was not done in this case. The day after the company eventually granted a disposition to the buyers, it went into receivership, and the disposition and the buyers' standard security for their own loan were not recorded until after that date. The receiver then claimed title to the flat as well as the right to keep the purchase price. This very unsatisfactory position from the point of view of the purchasers was held to be the correct one by both the Outer House and the Inner House of the Court of Session, despite the manifest unfairness, because, as at the date of the receivership, the company did still hold legal title to the flat. However, the House of Lords reversed the decision, and held that, as the company had no beneficial interest in the flat at the time of the crystallisation of the charge, since the whole purchase price had been paid, the floating charge did not attach to the flat on crystallisation and was not therefore available to the receiver. Great dissatisfaction with this decision was felt in Scotland, as it erodes the principle of faith in the public registers. Similar problems arose in cases in bankruptcy, but the outcomes were decided differently. The law has already been amended for personal bankruptcy in s 17 of the Bankruptcy and Diligence etc (Scotland) Act 2007, which introduces a grace period of 28 days for recording the disposition when a person buys heritable property from an individual or a partnership, during which, if the seller becomes bankrupt, the trustee in sequestration cannot claim the property. For companies, the Scottish Law Commission has proposed that the Bankruptcy and Diligence etc (Scotland) Act 2007 should be amended so that floating charges cannot attach to property until they have been publicised. The new register of floating charges under s 37 of the Bankruptcy and Diligence etc (Scotland) Act 2007 will also provide public knowledge of the date of creation of a floating charge, when that provision comes into force (see Chapter 13). The Scottish Law Commission also proposes that s 25 of the Titles to Land Consolidation (Scotland) Act 1868 should be amended so that a liquidator of an insolvent company would no longer be able immediately to complete title to heritable property, which the company has sold just prior to the liquidation, before the buyer has had time to record a disposition, to defeat the buyer's title. The Commission considers that further amendments are needed to the Insolvency Act 1986 so that buyers can find out earlier than at present whether a company is being put into liquidation. At the time of writing no decision has yet been reached on whether to adopt these proposals.

Administration

Administration was first introduced as part of big reforms to corporate insolvency law that took place in the mid-1980s with the purpose of trying to provide a better legal framework for the rescue of companies in financial distress. There was a major review of insolvency law carried out under the chairmanship of Sir Kenneth Cork, which reported in 1982. The Cork Report viewed receivership with considerable enthusiasm, and considered that creditors other than floating charge creditors should be allowed to enjoy its benefits. To achieve this, a new legal regime for the rescue of companies in financial distress – administration – was introduced. However, because administration needed a court order, it was really only suitable for very large companies. Since then, administration has been considerably revised by the Enterprise Act 2002, to make it available in some cases without obtaining a court order, and to put the focus more firmly on the rescue of companies. A timescale of 1 year was introduced to concentrate the minds of all those involved. As has been mentioned earlier in this chapter, the Enterprise Act 2002 also phased out receivership, with the effect that from 15 September 2003, floating charge creditors can no longer enforce their floating charges by the appointment of a receiver, but have to appoint an administrator instead, again to keep the focus on rescuing rather than breaking up companies. As recognition of the fact that creditors holding floating charges granted since 2003 no longer have the power to appoint receivers, they have been given the right to choose the person whom they wish to act as administrator.

The law on administration, unlike receivership, is the same for Scotland as for England and Wales. The law on administration is statutory and is found in s 8 of and Sch B1 to the Insolvency Act 1986.

In summary, a company in financial difficulty may be put into administration. A principal aim is to rescue it as a going concern, but it can also be used as an enforcement remedy by a floating charge creditor. An administrator is appointed (who must be a qualified insolvency practitioner), who takes over the running of the company from the directors, and may keep the company trading. The administrator works out a plan to achieve the purpose of the administration, which is approved by the creditors. The company then has a breathing space of a year during which creditors cannot enforce their claims against the company, to provide time for it to attempt to get back on its feet financially.

The purposes of administration

Administration has three purposes which are expressed in an order of priority in Sch B1, para 3:

- rescuing the company as a going concern, failing which
- achieving a better result for the company's creditors as a whole than would be likely if the company was wound up, failing which
- realising property in order to make a distribution to one or more of the preferential creditors.

The administrator must first try to achieve objective (a) and can only pursue (b) if (a) is thought not to be reasonably practicable or if pursuing (b) would provide a better result for the creditors as a whole. The administrator can only pursue objective (c) if he considers that neither (a) nor (b) is reasonably practicable, and that pursuing (c) does not unnecessarily harm the interests of the creditors as a whole.

Putting a company into administration without a court order

Since the enactment of the Enterprise Act 2002 it has been possible for the holder of a floating charge over all the company's assets and for the company itself and its directors to put the company into administration without any longer needing to obtain a court order.

Appointment by a floating charge creditor

For a floating charge holder to be able to appoint an administrator this way, the floating charge must state that the charge holder has the power to appoint an administrator or a receiver (who on appointment would be an administrative receiver) and the charge must relate to all or substantially all the company's property (a "qualifying floating charge"). If there is a provisional liquidator or a receiver in office, it is not competent for a floating charge creditor to appoint an administrator in this way. Two days' written notice of the intention to appoint an administrator must be given to the holder of any prior ranking floating charge, unless the holder of any such charge has consented to the proposed appointment. The actual appointment is made by written notice of appointment in the prescribed form, which is filed with the court. It names the floating charge creditor's choice of administrator, who must indicate in the notice of appointment his consent, and that, in his opinion, the purposes of the administration are reasonably likely to be achieved. The administration commences on the date of filing the application at court.

Appointment by the company or its directors

Both the company and its directors may appoint an administrator without obtaining a court order (para 22 of Sch B1). However, this is not allowed if the company has previously been in administration in the past 12 months, as otherwise a company could be allowed to stagger from one administration to another and have permanent shelter from its creditors. It is also not competent if a petition has been presented for a winding-up order, which is still pending, or if it is a company where receivership is permitted and a receiver has taken office. The company or its directors must serve notice of intention to appoint an administrator of 5 business days on the holder of any floating charge. The actual appointment of an administrator is done by a notice of appointment which is filed with the court (as discussed above for an appointment of an administrator by a floating charge creditor). Again, the proposed administrator must state his consent, and also that, in his opinion, the purposes of the administration are reasonably likely to be achieved. The administration commences on the date of filing the application at court.

Appointment of an administrator by the court

This used to be the only way a company could be put into administration, which made the whole process slow and expensive. It is still competent to seek an administration order, and for creditors other than a floating charge creditor with the new "qualifying floating charge" this is the only method. This is also the only form of administration available to some special types of company including water companies, railway companies, public–private partnership companies, and building societies (some of which are still entitled to appoint receivers, as discussed earlier in this chapter). If there are international aspects to the administration, a court order may be necessary, in order to provide for cross-border enforcement.

To obtain an administration order, it has to be proved to the court that the company is insolvent or is likely to become so, and that it is reasonably likely to achieve the purposes of the administration.

The same purposes of administration apply where a court order is sought as where it is obtained without court order. Where an administration order is sought, two requirements must be met before the court will grant the order:

- the company is or is likely to be unable to pay its debts, and
- the administration order is reasonably likely to achieve the purpose of administration (para 11 of Sch B1). The purposes of administration, in descending order of priority, are provided in para 3 of Sch B1 (set out earlier in this chapter).

The legal effects of administration – paras 40–45 of Sch B1

The legal effects of administration are as follows:

- with a few exceptions, notably winding up in the public interest, if the company has been put into administration by the holder of a floating charge, any petition to wind up the company is suspended for the duration of the administration;
- any receiver who has been appointed must vacate office;
- there is a period of 1 year from the commencement of the administration during which there is a moratorium or temporary ban on the following;
  - no resolution may be passed or (with a few exceptions) court order made for the winding up of the company;
  - no steps may be taken to enforce any security or repossess any hire purchase goods against the company except with the consent of the administrator or the court;
  - a landlord may not exercise a right of irritancy on a lease in relation to premises let, except with the consent of the administrator or the court;
  - no legal process may be begun or continued against the company or its property, except with the consent of the administrator or the court.

The purpose of this moratorium is to provide time for a survival plan to be worked out for the company under the direction of the administrator and for it to be put into effect. To some extent, this may put a company at some competitive advantage over other businesses in the market, as creditors cannot enforce their claims. In the world of football, one way of dealing with this competitive advantage has been to impose a deduction of a substantial number of points in a league competition when a football club is put into administration.

There is no similar moratorium when a company goes into receivership, with the effect that a company in receivership would often struggle to stay in business, as creditors, once they are aware that the company is in some degree of financial difficulty, will lose no time in enforcing their claims.

Creditors of a company in administration have applied to the court at times, asking it to disapply the moratorium, to allow them to enforce their claims. In such cases the court has to balance the interests of creditors against those of the company. The leading case is *Re Atlantic Computer Systems plc* (1992), in which the funders of computer equipment which the company in administration leased to its customers, sought the court's permission to enforce their rights, as the company was receiving rental but not paying the funders anything. The Court of Appeal held that this was a case in which it should exercise its discretion to allow enforcement by the funders, as otherwise the funders were going to suffer at the expense of other creditors. This case laid out guidelines for future courts to use in deciding whether the leave of the court should be granted, which have been approved in the Scottish case of *Scottish Exhibition Centre Ltd v Minestrop Ltd (in Administration) (No 2)* (1996).

Duties of the administrator

The administrator immediately sends notice of appointment to the company and makes his appointment public, sending notice to Companies House within 7 days. He also writes to all the company's known creditors. With the help of the directors and other employees, the administrator prepares a statement of affairs showing details of all the creditors and their claims and securities and all the company's assets.

Once an administrator has taken office, he must immediately take stock of the company's financial position, as we saw previously in the case of the receiver. Just like the receiver, an administrator may have to take some rapid decisions such as whether the company should continue to trade, and whether the company or part of it should be sold. The administrator has to prepare proposals within 2 months of taking office, as to how the particular statutory purpose that is the subject of that administration is to be achieved (para 49 of Sch B1). We have already seen earlier in this chapter that these purposes are, in order: the rescue of the company as a going concern, a better result for the creditors than would be achieved by putting the company into liquidation, and the realisation of the company's property to make a return to the company's secured or preferential creditors. These proposals may include seeking a company voluntary arrangement under Pt I of the Insolvency Act 1986 (discussed briefly later in this chapter), or seeking a compromise or arrangement under Pt 26 of the Companies Act 2006, which will be discussed in Chapter 16. The proposals can be thought of as a business plan to achieve the purpose sought. A copy of the proposals is then notified to Companies House and sent to all known creditors and members as soon as possible and, at the latest, by the end of 8 weeks from the commencement of the administration. The proposals are then put before a meeting of the creditors and voted on. The creditors' vote is determined according to the amount of each creditor's debt. The administrator has a duty to manage the company's property in accordance with the proposals (para 68 of Sch B1).

Powers and liability of administrator

Depending on what the proposals entail, the administrator may have to gather in the company's property with a view to paying creditors. Unlike a receiver, an administrator is an officer of the company. The administrator has various statutory powers which are set out in Sch 1 to the Insolvency Act 1986, which include the power to gather in the company's property, and to raise court proceedings to do so, and also the power to raise money and borrow money on security. The administrator has the power to make any arrangement or compromise on behalf of the company, by para 18 of Sch 1, which allows him to pay creditors. The administrator has the powers to run the business by para 14 of Sch 1, and the directors, though still in office, are not permitted to exercise any management powers except with the consent of the administrator under para 64 of Sch B1. The administrator has the power to appoint and remove directors under para 61 of Sch B1. When the administrator contracts on behalf of the company, third parties who contract in good faith and for value can rely on the fact that the administrator is acting within his powers.

When an administrator contracts on behalf of the company in administration, and incurs new credit, those creditors assume a priority for payment ahead of the administrator's own remuneration and expenses and over any floating charge creditor, by virtue of para 99(4) of Sch B1. This also applies to certain claims by employees of the company for work done during the period when the administrator is in office (para 99(5)). In the case of those employees, in a similar way to work done by employees during a receivership described earlier in this chapter, an administrator has a 14-day grace period to decide which employees should be retained. If employees are asked to continue to work beyond that period, their contracts are deemed to have been adopted by the administrator. They will have a super-priority for wages or salary (including holiday pay, sick pay and contributions to an occupational pension scheme) over the administrator's own claims for remuneration and expenses and ahead of the claim of a floating charge creditor.

Redundancy and unfair dismissal payments were held in the case of *Re Allders Department Stores Ltd (in Administration)* (2005) not to have priority over the administrator's remuneration and expenses, on the basis that they are not wages or salary.

Unlike the receiver, the administrator does not contract with personal liability.

In the recent case of *Nortel GmbH and Others* (2010), the court held that the collapsed companies in the Lehman Brothers and Nortel groups had to contribute funds to the occupational pension schemes of their associated companies because pension fund deficits were held to be an expense of the administration rather than a debt due by the companies. This meant that the payments would take priority over other creditors. The judgment, which is very good news for pension creditors but less so for other creditors, is likely to be appealed.

The administrator's powers also include the power to sell assets and to put the company into liquidation. By para 70 of Sch B1, the administrator has power to dispose of property which is subject to a floating charge, on the basis that the holder of the charge will acquire the same priority in the proceeds of sale as in the original property subject to the charge. The administrator may also dispose of property which is subject to a fixed security under para 71, but in this case there must be an application to the court, which must approve the disposal as being likely to promote the purpose of the administration. Also, the proceeds of the disposal must be used towards discharging the sum secured. A similar procedure applies to the realisation of goods subject to hire purchase under para 72.

Unlike receivership and liquidation, where there is a statutory ranking order, in the case of administration, the settlement of creditors' claims may be done in the course of fulfilment of the proposals, but is not a formal stage of the process. Different companies may be in very different financial circumstances. However, depending on what the purpose of the administration is, the administrator is likely to have to settle with creditors and there are some restrictions on how this is done. The administrator has power to make a distribution to a secured or preferential creditor under para 65 of Sch B1. In that event, the same rules on payment of preferential creditors ranking before floating charge creditors apply in regard to a company in administration as is the case of a company in receivership or a company in liquidation, as described elsewhere in this chapter. If a distribution to any other class of creditor is to be made, the consent of the court needs to be obtained. However, para 66 grants the administrator power to make payments to other classes of creditors without the permission of the court if he considers it is likely to assist the achievement of the purposes of the administration. There is also a general power to the administrator under para 13 of Sch 1 to make a payment which is necessary or incidental to the performance of the administrator's functions. He also has power to compromise claims under para 18 of Sch 1. By para 99 of Sch B1, the administrator's own remuneration and expenses are paid in priority to a floating charge creditor.

An administrator, like a liquidator, has power to challenge in court certain antecedent transactions that took place in the run-up to an administration. These challenges are to gratuitous alienations, unfair preferences, extortionate credit transactions and certain floating charges. These will be discussed in relation to liquidation in Chapter 15, but are equally relevant to administration. Also, an administrator, like a liquidator, can challenge acts of the directors and others as being in breach of duty or as fraudulent trading or wrongful trading with a view to seeking a contribution to the assets of the company in order to pay creditors. These provisions of the Insolvency Act 1986 will also be discussed in Chapter 15 in relation to liquidation, but, again, apply equally to administration.

Protection of the interests of creditors and members

The administrator clearly has considerable power over the company's property, and this might be open to abuse. To counter this, there are some protections for members and creditors. The administrator must convene a creditors' meeting if requested to do so by the holders of 10 per cent in value of the creditors under para 56 of Sch B1. The court also has power to order a creditors' meeting.

Also, any member or creditor has the power to petition the court under para 74 of Sch B1 on the ground that the administrator is acting unfairly or is not carrying out his duties quickly or efficiently enough. The court has discretionary powers to make an order on such a petition, but it cannot do so if it would interfere with a voluntary arrangement under Pt I of the Insolvency Act 1986 or a compromise or arrangement under Pt 26 of the Companies Act 2006, a cross-border merger or a proposal or modified proposal approved by the creditors more than 28 days prior to the petition to court.

What happens at the end of an administration

The changes to administration brought about by the Enterprise Act 2002 were designed to inject some urgency into administration, as the longer the process dragged on, the less likely companies were to be rescued successfully. Therefore, an administration will come to an end automatically at the end of a year, unless the period is extended for a further 6 months, on application to the court, with the consent of each secured creditor and more than 50 per cent of the unsecured creditors, under para 76 of Sch B1.

The administrator may also apply to the court to end the administration early under para 79, if he considers that the purpose of the administration cannot be achieved or he considers the company should not have entered administration.

If the administrator has been appointed by the holder of a floating charge, by the company itself or by its directors, the administrator has power to bring the administration to an end without the approval of the court if he considers that the objective of the administration has been achieved. This is done by filing notice with the court and notifying all creditors under para 80.

A creditor also has the power to bring an administration to an end, by petitioning the court on the ground that the person who sought the appointment of the administrator had an improper motive for doing so, in terms of para 81.

In the course of the administration the company may become insolvent if it was not already insolvent before the process started, or it may become evident that the company has no future. In such a case the administrator may advise the members to pass a resolution to put the company into voluntary liquidation. This may be done under para 83 where the administrator considers that each secured creditor will receive payment of his debt and a distribution will be made to any unsecured creditors. Also, an administration would also come to an end if the company is wound up in the public interest under s 124A of the Insolvency Act 1986 or under various other statutory provisions.

An administration would also come to an end on the dissolution of the company without winding up, under para 84. Dissolution may be used where it is not worth while putting a company into liquidation, and will be discussed in Chapter 15.

Ceasing office as administrator

A person has limited rights to resign the office of administrator under r 2.49 of the Insolvency (Scotland) Rules 1986. An administrator may be removed from office and another administrator appointed in his place by the holder of a floating charge or by the directors of the company under paras 92 and 93 of Sch B1. If there is more than one qualifying floating charge, and an administrator is appointed by the holder of a floating charge where there is another prior ranking floating charge in existence, the holder of that prior ranking floating charge may remove the administrator and insist on appointing his personal choice of administrator under para 96.

When an administrator ceases office, he will be discharged from liability as specified in para 98 of Sch B1.

Pre-pack administration

When a company goes into administration, it puts it on the public record that a company is in some degree of financial difficulty. The directors will be aware of the state of the company's finances long before this. It may be easier for the directors to cut a deal for the rescue of the company when negotiations can take place privately. One possibility is to use what has come to be called "pre-pack" administration, whereby the directors have quietly lined up a buyer for the business before the company is put into administration. This may enable a sale to take place at a better price as more goodwill may be preserved, and more jobs may be saved. Often companies are sold to the incumbent management in this way, and there has been some concern about whether best value for the creditors is achieved, as the directors may have a conflict of interest, and there might be better offers for the company or its assets on the market. A pre-pack administration may enable a business to be sold to the incumbent management free of debt, leaving its unsecured creditors with nothing. Where part of the business is sold, some creditors (and particularly the government, which is no longer a preferential creditor) may be left high and dry as creditors of the rump of the now insolvent company.

Pre-pack administrations are very common, and it is estimated that a third of all administrations in 2009 were pre-packs.

There is concern about the lack of transparency in some of these cases, where creditors are presented with a done deal. As most administrations nowadays take place without application to the court, the opportunity for court scrutiny of pre-packs is limited. *Re Kayley Vending Ltd* (2009) was a case where an administration order was sought in connection with a pre-pack sale of a cigarette vending machine business which had failed largely as a consequence of the smoking ban in pubs. The court commented on its role in relation to pre-packs, which it saw as being to ensure that the administration process was not being obviously abused to the disadvantage of the creditors.

The Insolvency Service issued a consultation paper in 2010 about whether more regulation of pre-pack administrations might be appropriate. Suggestions in that paper include requiring creditor or court approval to a sale of a business in administration to connected parties and requiring a different insolvency practitioner to sign off the pre-pack sale to ensure a greater degree of objectivity. However, both these suggestions would tend to defeat the object of a pre-pack administration in ensuring a rapid sale and preservation of the jobs of the workforce.

Company voluntary arrangements

The company voluntary arrangement is another legal regime whose main aim, like administration, is to rescue a company that is in financial difficulty. An example of a recent fairly successful company voluntary arrangement is the company JJB Sports in 2009, under which rental claims on closed stores were compromised and rental terms on remaining stores were changed, allowing the company to avoid going into administration at that time. At the time of writing, JJB Sports has entered a second company voluntary arrangement. Often a company will go into administration with the purpose of entering a company voluntary arrangement. This section of the chapter gives a very brief overview of the company voluntary arrangement. The situation is complicated by the fact that there are two regimes: one applies to all companies and another is for small companies only, which includes a short moratorium of 28 days during which the creditors cannot enforce their claims against the company.

The rules for the company voluntary arrangement are found in ss 1–7 of the Insolvency Act 1986 (the regime for all companies) and Sch A1 to the Insolvency Act 1986 (the regime for small companies). The rules apply to England and Wales and to Scotland but not to Northern Ireland.

The company voluntary arrangement regime for all companies must be supervised by a qualified insolvency practitioner, whereas the regime for small companies allows suitably qualified professionals without this qualification to hold office under s 1(2) of the Insolvency Act 1986.

In a voluntary arrangement, a proposal is made to the company and its creditors for a composition in satisfaction of its debts or a scheme of arrangement of its affairs (s 1(1)). In a company voluntary arrangement, there might, for example, be a rescheduling of the company's debts, or a swap of debt for equity, in the hope that it might lead to the survival of the company. However, a voluntary arrangement is not allowed to interfere with the rights of secured or preferential creditors, except with their concurrence (s 4 of the Insolvency Act 1986).

Under s 1, a proposal for a voluntary arrangement can be made by the company's directors, by an administrator if the company is in administration, and by a liquidator if the company is in liquidation. The proposal will nominate a particular person to be the eventual supervisor of the arrangement. If the company is already in administration or liquidation, the administrator or liquidator may act as the supervisor.

Where the nominee is not the current administrator or liquidator, the nominee will examine the proposed scheme and will report to the court on its likely prospects of success. Where the nominee is either the administrator or the liquidator there is no need to report to the court. In all cases the nominee will then summon separate meetings of creditors and members, which must decide whether or not to approve the voluntary arrangement. The consent required is a simple majority of the members in value and three-quarters or more in value of the creditors (rr 1.16A and 1.16B of the Insolvency (Scotland) Rules 1986). If the two groups do not agree, the wishes of the creditors prevail, although the members have the right to challenge this in court.

As already mentioned, the directors of certain companies are allowed to seek a short moratorium of 28 days from the date when documents are filed at court, ending with the date when the later of the meetings of creditors and members is held (para 8 of Sch A1). To be eligible, the company must be a small private company, as defined for accounting purposes by s 382 of the Companies Act 2006, it must not be a bank, building society or insurance company or certain other special types of company, it must not already be subject to formal insolvency procedures and it must not have had a failed moratorium in the past 12 months. The purpose of the moratorium is to allow a short time for the scheme to be thought out properly, free from pressure from creditors.

The effect of the moratorium is similar to that explained in administration.

After the arrangement has been approved, by s 5 of the Insolvency Act 1986, it binds every member and creditor who would have been entitled to vote, even if they did not vote, and also binds the company. However, the voluntary arrangement can be challenged by any member or creditor by application to the court on one of two grounds:

- the interests of a member or creditor have been unfairly prejudiced by the arrangement, or
- there has been a material irregularity at or in relation to either of the meetings (s 6).

In the case of a small company with a moratorium, any creditor, director, or member of the company or any other person affected by the moratorium has the power to apply to the court if dissatisfied by any act or omission of the nominee during the moratorium, by para 26.

There is also power to challenge the supervisor's implementation of the proposal, by application to court by creditors and others under s 7.

Once the voluntary arrangement has been approved any moratorium ceases and the creditors may once again enforce their claims. The nominee becomes the supervisor at this point and must monitor the implementation of the scheme. It is important to remember that with a company voluntary arrangement, unlike administration, the directors continue to run the company (debtor in possession). The supervisor must present accounts annually to creditors and report to the company on the scheme's progress by r 1.21A of the Insolvency (Scotland) Rules 1986.

Neither form of company voluntary arrangement has been as much used as administration. At the time of writing there is a government proposal from 2009 to provide a moratorium in a company voluntary arrangement to all companies, and this was broadly welcomed by respondents, and the government proposes to take this further.

Essential Facts

- The purposes behind corporate insolvency law are to rescue businesses that are viable, and, where businesses are not viable, to pay creditors in a way society considers fair, all the while seeking to protect the public from unscrupulous traders.
- The various regimes of corporate insolvency law are: receivership, administration, the company voluntary arrangement, and both voluntary and compulsory liquidation.

- In almost every case, the person in charge of each of these regimes must be a qualified insolvency practitioner.

- Receivership is a remedy to the holder of a floating charge which allows the holder to appoint a receiver to realise the asset or assets subject to the floating charge for the benefit of the creditor. There are other creditors who have to be paid first. For floating charges granted since the Enterprise Act 2002 came into force, receivership is not generally available.

- Administration is a regime primarily intended to rescue a company which is in financial difficulties. An administrator takes charge of the company. Since the Enterprise Act 2002, it is also the way in which floating charge creditors enforce their security over company assets.

- A pre-pack administration is an administration that has been worked out in advance before the regime becomes public knowledge.

- A company voluntary arrangement is another means of rescuing a company in financial difficulties, but in this case the directors continue to run the company under supervision.

Essential Cases

Cuckmere Brick Co Ltd v Mutual Finance Ltd (1971): it was held in this English case that if a receiver decides to sell property subject to a floating charge, he owes the company a duty of reasonable care to try to obtain a reasonable price in a sale of the company's property.

Independent Pension Trustee Ltd v LAW Construction Co Ltd (1997): where assets subject to a floating charge are under the control of the receiver, the directors are not allowed to exercise control of the same assets.

Armour v Thyssen Edelstahlwerke AG (1990): where a supplier had supplied goods to a company under a retention of title clause which retained title until all sums due on that and also other contracts had been paid, it was held by the House of Lords that that was a valid sale under ss 17 and 19 of the Sale of Goods Act 1979, rather than, as had been previously thought, an invalid attempt to create a security over moveable goods without handing over possession, which is incompetent in Scotland.

Sharp v Thomson (1997): a company sold heritable property (land and buildings) and went into receivership before the buyers had had an opportunity to record the disposition in their favour, although the price had been paid – it was held in the House of Lords that as the company no longer had beneficial ownership once the price was paid, the floating charge should be deemed not to have attached to the flat, and it was not therefore available to the receiver. It is proposed that the law should be changed so that floating charges should not attach to property until their existence has been publicised.

Re Atlantic Computer Systems plc (1992): the Court of Appeal provided some guidance on the circumstances in which it might be appropriate for a court to grant leave to lift the effect of the moratorium in administration: it might be appropriate to allow a landlord or hirer of goods to repossess them if it was unlikely to harm the purposes of administration; in other cases the court would have to balance the interests of the company and the creditors in deciding.

Re Allders Department Stores Ltd (in Administration) (2005): the employee's priority over the payment of the administrator's remuneration and expenses does not extend to redundancy and unfair dismissal payments.

Nortel GmbH and Others (2010): where a company in administration owed money to occupational pension schemes of associated companies, such payments were an expense of the administration and not a debt due by the company. This meant that they were payable ahead of other creditors, and the pension claimants were more likely to receive some payment.

Re Kayley Vending Ltd (2009): in a pre-pack administration where a court order is sought, the role of the court is to ensure that the administration process is not being obviously abused to the detriment of the creditors.

15 CORPORATE INSOLVENCY: WINDING UP

LIQUIDATION

Liquidation (also called winding up), is a different kind of process to those described in the last chapter. With liquidation, the affairs of a company are brought to a close. This may be because the company is no longer needed, or it may be because it is insolvent, or because it is harming the interests of the public. In the liquidation process, a liquidator is appointed who must be a qualified insolvency practitioner. The company's assets are gathered in, and creditors are paid insofar as there is money to do so. If there are any spare assets at that point, they are returned to the members. Once the whole process is finished, the company will be dissolved and its name removed from the register at Companies House.

The statutory rules on liquidation are found in Pt IV of the Insolvency Act 1986. Many of the rules are identical for England and Wales and Scotland, although there are some differences as some of the rules originate in the law of bankruptcy, where there are differences.

Liquidation can be *voluntary* (by a resolution of the members) or *compulsory* (by court order).

Voluntary liquidation

A voluntary liquidation must be initiated by a resolution of the members of the company. By s 84 of the Insolvency Act 1986, this can either be by an ordinary resolution, if the articles of association provide that the company is to be wound up on the occurrence of a particular event or the expiry of a certain time, or by special resolution if the members wish the company to be wound up for any reason. A special resolution is therefore the default method for winding up a company voluntarily.

A voluntary liquidation can be either a members' voluntary liquidation or a creditors' voluntary liquidation.

Members' voluntary liquidation

In a members' voluntary liquidation, the directors make a statutory declaration that the company will be able to pay all its debts in full with interest within 12 months of the start of the winding up. That statutory declaration, together with a statement of the company's assets and liabilities, is registered at Companies House under s 89. There are criminal penalties for directors who make a statutory declaration without having reasonable grounds for the opinion stated therein on the company's solvency. In a members' voluntary liquidation, the creditors have the comfort of knowing they will be paid in full, and consequently they have a smaller role in the supervision of the liquidation process. In this kind of liquidation, the liquidator is chosen by the members only.

Creditors' voluntary liquidation

A creditors' voluntary liquidation is a liquidation in which there is no declaration of solvency (s 90). If the circumstances of a company in members' voluntary liquidation change and it becomes clear that the company is insolvent, the liquidation will be converted to a creditors' voluntary liquidation. In a creditors' voluntary liquidation, the company is insolvent, which means that not all creditors will be paid in full. Consequently, the creditors are involved in supervising the liquidation process to make sure that it is done fairly.

In a creditors' voluntary liquidation, the company must call a meeting of creditors within 14 days of the date of the resolution to wind up the company (s 98). Creditors must be given a full statement of the company's affairs at the meeting. Both the creditors' meeting and the general meeting may choose a person to be the liquidator of the company, but if they do not agree, the creditors' choice prevails by virtue of s 100. The members and creditors may also appoint a liquidation committee of up to five persons each, to advise and supervise the liquidator, though the creditors have power to object to the members' choice unless the court otherwise orders (s 101).

It will be remembered that when a company goes into receivership or administration, the powers of the directors are suspended, although they remain in office. In the case of a company subject to a company voluntary arrangement, the directors continue to run the company under supervision. However, when a company goes into members' voluntary liquidation, by s 91(2) the powers of the directors cease except insofar as they are sanctioned by the company in general meeting or by the liquidator. Similarly, in the case of creditors' voluntary liquidation, by s 103 the powers of the directors cease except where they are sanctioned by the liquidation committee or by the creditors. The affairs of the company are run from now on by the liquidator. Generally the business does not continue to run when a company goes into voluntary liquidation, except perhaps for a short time.

Compulsory liquidation

Compulsory liquidation occurs when a company is wound up by order of the court. In Scotland, by s 120, petitions can be presented to the Court of Session and also to the sheriff court of the sheriffdom in which the company's registered office is situated if the paid-up share capital of the company does not exceed £120,000.

The following parties have the legal standing to bring a petition for compulsory liquidation under s 124:

- the company itself, or its directors;
- the Official Receiver (England and Wales, but not Scotland);
- the Department for Business, Innovation and Skills, acting in the public interest, following an investigation, or where a public company has failed to obtain a trading certificate;
- a contributory (member);
- a creditor or creditors.

Also, under other statutory grounds, the following may petition:

- a receiver (where still permitted) or an administrator, if the company is insolvent, under Sch 1, para 21.

Grounds on which compulsory liquidation may be sought

By ss 122 and 124A of the Insolvency Act 1986, the grounds for a petition for compulsory liquidation are:

- the company has passed a special resolution that it should be wound up by the court (which would be rare, since the company could do this by voluntary liquidation without going to court);
- the company was registered as a public company, but has not been issued with a trading certificate under s 761 of the Companies Act 2006 by the end of one year;
- the company has not commenced business within a year, or has suspended its business for a year or more;
- the number of members of the company has dropped below two in companies to which that rule still applies;
- the company is unable to pay its debts, as defined in s 123 of the Insolvency Act 1986, which will be discussed below;
- a small private company has had a moratorium of 28 days in order to propose a company voluntary arrangement, as discussed earlier in

this chapter, and the moratorium has come to an end without the company voluntary arrangement coming into effect (which allows the creditors to petition for compulsory liquidation);

- the court is of the opinion that it is just and equitable for the company to be wound up (discussed in Chapter 11);

- the Department for Business, Innovation and Skills is of the opinion that it is expedient that the company be wound up in the public interest. This allows the government to seek to wind up fraudulent companies that prey on the public;

- there is a floating charge over the company's property, and the court is satisfied that the charge holder's security is in jeopardy, because in the circumstances there are fears that the company might dispose of its property to the prejudice of the floating charge creditor. This ground applies to Scotland only.

When is a company unable to pay its debts?

This is the most usual ground for seeking a compulsory liquidation, and it would be initiated by a creditor or creditors. In principle, a company may be put into liquidation when it is perfectly able to pay its debts, but simply fails to do so. Often the process is initiated, but the company fairly promptly does pay its debts. Under s 123, a company is deemed to be unable to pay its debts in the following circumstances:

- it has failed to pay a debt of more than £750 within 3 weeks of receiving a written demand for payment from the creditor. Copies of the creditors' paperwork relating to this demand constitute the evidence of inability to pay the debt;

- a creditor has obtained a court decree (judgment) for the debt and the time period has elapsed after which the creditor would be able to enforce the decree, without the debt being discharged; also, on the lapse of a time period in certain cases where enforcement is permissible without a court decree, such as a protested bill of exchange or a bond which is registered for execution in the Books of Council and Session (one of the public registers);

- it is proved to the satisfaction of the court that the company is unable to pay its debts as they fall due;

- it is proved to the satisfaction of the court that the value of the company's assets is less than the value of its liabilities (absolute insolvency).

Who is likely to petition and on what grounds?

The various grounds of compulsory liquidation would be used by different interest groups. If the members of the company can command the appropriate majority, they would generally prefer to put the company into voluntary liquidation rather than seeking compulsory liquidation. Members would only use compulsory liquidation if voluntary liquidation is not open to them. Minority members might seek to wind up the company on the ground that it is just and equitable to do so, as explained in Chapter 11.

A "contributory" is a person who is liable to contribute to the assets of a company in liquidation. That might be a shareholder who holds partly paid shares, a member of a company limited by guarantee, or a member of an unlimited company (ss 74–76 of the Insolvency Act 1986). By s 124, there are various restrictions on a contributory's right to petition. In most cases a contributory is allowed to petition for the compulsory liquidation of a company only if the shares were originally allotted to him or if he has held the shares for at least 6 out of the previous 18 months or has inherited them. This is to try to prevent vexatious petitions by people who buy shares in order to liquidate a company. By s 125, a court may refuse to allow a contributory to petition to have the company wound up on the just and equitable ground if there is another remedy available (such as a petition based on unfairly prejudicial conduct – ss 994–998 of the Companies Act 2006) and the court considers that the use of winding up on this ground is unreasonable.

Among these possible petitioners, unsecured creditors are the most likely to petition on the ground that the company cannot pay its debts. Secured creditors can protect themselves by enforcing their securities. An unsecured creditor will only resort to liquidation where the creditor has evidence that the company has sufficient assets to cover the prior ranking creditors and also the petitioner's debt. It would be pointless to waste money on putting the company into liquidation otherwise.

The procedure for a petition for a winding-up order

Once a petition is presented to court, there is an opportunity for the company to respond and lodge answers – in other words, to defend itself. Often the debt will be paid at this point if it is a petition related to the non-payment of debt.

During the time between the presenting of the petition and the granting of a winding-up order, in some companies the creditors may justifiably fear that assets might disappear and evidence of misconduct by directors might be destroyed. In such cases it is possible to seek the appointment of a *provisional liquidator* under s 134 to act as a temporary guardian of the company's affairs until a liquidator can be appointed.

The procedural rules for the conduct of a liquidation in Scotland are found in a statutory instrument – the Insolvency (Scotland) Rules 1986 (SI 1986/1915).

If a company is put into compulsory liquidation, the date of commencement of the liquidation is backdated to the date of the presentation of the petition to the court by s 129 of the Insolvency Act 1986. That is an important date, as some people may be made to contribute financially to the pot of money available to pay the creditors because of various acts that were done in the run-up to the liquidation, and various time limits apply, as will be seen later in this chapter. The clock in relation to all those time limits runs backwards from the date of the commencement of the liquidation. The idea behind these rules is to prevent unfairness to the general body of creditors.

The procedure for putting a company into liquidation involves considerable publicity. Both the fact of the petition and the granting of the order must be notified to Companies House and advertised in newspapers circulating in the areas where the company is based.

When the court grants the winding-up order, in Scotland the court will appoint an *interim liquidator* under s 138, to hold office until the liquidator is appointed. His role is to call meetings of creditors and contributories so that the liquidator can be chosen. In England, the Official Receiver fulfils that role. At this point the interim liquidator will examine the financial state of the company by calling for a statement of affairs to be prepared. There is power for the officers of the company to be publicly examined in court, and there are powers for creditors and contributories to request this under s 133.

The choice of the liquidator is made at meetings of creditors and contributories. In the event of the two meetings nominating a different person, the creditors' choice would prevail under s 139.

A liquidation committee may be set up in both a creditors' voluntary liquidation (s 101) and a compulsory liquidation (s 142). The purpose of this committee is to advise and supervise the liquidator. Some of the powers of the liquidator have to be approved, and, as will be seen, this approval can be given by the liquidation committee or the court.

The legal effects of a compulsory winding up

- As has already been mentioned, the date of commencement of the liquidation is backdated to the date of the presentation of the petition under s 129. That date applies to all the following legal effects.

- The company can do very little from now on, as s 127 states that any dispositions of company property, or transfer of shares, or alteration in the status of the company's members, made after the commencement of the winding up are void unless the court otherwise orders.

- The winding-up order operates as a very powerful diligence, and has an effect on the use of diligence by creditors. Under s 128, creditors may no longer use diligence to enforce their claims against the company from the date of commencement of the liquidation, and any such diligence would be void. "Diligence" is a technical term that refers to the enforcement of claims against a debtor so as to give the creditor rights in security over assets of the debtor. This legal effect is then extended backwards by s 185, which borrows from the law of personal bankruptcy in Scotland and states that any diligence done within 60 days prior to the date of commencement of the liquidation is made void. The reason for this is to try to be fair to the body of creditors, and not allow a few, who perhaps had more knowledge of the company's affairs than the rest, to take unfair advantage. Any creditors who have used diligence within this 60-day period will have to hand back to the liquidator any money or assets they have gained through doing so, though where the diligence is over a particular asset they do have a preference for their *bona fide* expenses out of the proceeds of the sale of the asset.

- No legal action may be begun or continued against the company, except with the leave of the court (s 130).

- The assets of the company remain vested in the company as a legal person, though controlled by the liquidator. However, the liquidator can request the court to order all or any part of the company's property to vest in the liquidator, which would put the title to the company's property into the liquidator's name (s 145).

- In relation to contracts of employment, the judgment in the case of *Day* v *Tait* (1900) has been thought to suggest that a winding-up order could be treated as a repudiatory breach of the contract of employment by the company. (This is discussed by John St Clair and James Drummond Young in *The Law of Corporate Insolvency in Scotland* (3rd edn, 2004) at 298.)

- In contrast to the position when a company goes into receivership or administration, where the powers of the directors are suspended, in the case of a company in compulsory liquidation the powers of the directors cease, except insofar as they are sanctioned by the liquidation committee or by the creditors (s 103). The directors do have certain duties imposed on them, such as the duty to prepare a statement of affairs.

- If there is a floating charge, liquidation is one of the events that would cause the floating charge to become fixed, as discussed in Chapter 13. Currently, this provision is still found in s 463 of the Companies Act 1985, but it will soon be replaced by s 45 of the Bankruptcy and Diligence etc (Scotland) Act 2007. Usually, liquidation would preclude the appointment of an administrator in both a compulsory liquidation and a voluntary liquidation under para 8 of Sch B1 to the Insolvency Act 1986. However, there is an exception for the holder of a qualifying floating charge granted after the Enterprise Act 2002 came into force in 2003 to apply to the court for an administration order under para 37 of Sch B1, which, if granted, discharges the winding-up order and allows an administration to take place.

The powers of the liquidator – both voluntary liquidation and compulsory liquidation

The liquidator's task is to gather in the assets of the company, pay the creditors in a fixed order of priority, and then, if there is any surplus, pay it to the members. The liquidator has statutory powers under the Insolvency Act 1986, s 165 (for voluntary liquidation), and s 167 (for compulsory liquidation) and Sch 4. These powers include the power to raise actions, power to compromise claims with creditors, power to sell the company's assets and power to borrow money on the security of the company's assets. Although the liquidator has power to run the company's business, this power extends only as far as is necessary for the beneficial winding up of the company. Some of these powers need to be sanctioned. In the case of a members' voluntary liquidation, this approval comes from the members by special resolution. In a creditors' voluntary liquidation the approval is by the court or by a liquidation committee if there is one, or, if not, by the creditors. In a compulsory liquidation, the approval is by the court or the liquidation committee.

Gathering in the company's assets

It is the task of the liquidator to work to maximise the assets for the benefit of the creditors. This may involve selling the business (or more likely part of the business) as a going concern, and selling assets. The liquidator may have to resort to raising actions in the civil courts.

The liquidator has the power to challenge certain transactions that took place prior to the commencement of the liquidation, in order to recover money or property that can be used to pay creditors. These are: (i) *gratuitous alienations* (s 242); (ii) *unfair preferences* (s 243); (iii) *extortionate credit transactions* (s 244); and (iv) *invalid floating charges* (s 245).

(1) *Gratuitous alienations* under s 242 are transactions in which the company has given away its property free of charge or sold it at an undervalue, or has waived a rightful claim. This provision only applies to Scotland. A transaction is challengeable in court if it took place within 2 years prior to the commencement of the liquidation, which is increased to 5 years if the transaction was in favour of somebody associated with the company. The challenge can be brought by a liquidator, by an administrator of a company in administration, and by a creditor. If successful, the transaction can be reduced by the court, so that the property has to be returned to the company. However, the transaction will not be reduced if the person who received the asset can prove one of the following:

(a) at the time of or after the alienation, the company's assets were greater than its liabilities;

(b) the transaction can be shown to have been made for adequate consideration (which does not have to be full market value);

(c) The alienation was a reasonable birthday, Christmas or other conventional gift, or a charitable gift to a person not connected to the company.

If a third party has acquired the assets in good faith and for value from the person who received the asset from the company, the rights of that party are unaffected (s 242(6)).

Following a successful challenge of a gratuitous alienation, the party who has to hand back the asset is in the unfortunate position of becoming a postponed creditor by virtue of r 4.66(2)(a) of the Insolvency (Scotland) Rules 1986, which will be discussed later in this chapter.

An "associate" for the purposes on this section includes other companies in a group, controlling shareholders, directors, employees, and various relatives of these persons as defined in s 435.

In *Jackson* v *Royal Bank of Scotland* (2002), the bank had granted group overdraft facilities backed by inter-company guarantees to a group of four companies, three of which were insolvent. The fourth company went into liquidation, at which point the bank called up the guarantee. The liquidator challenged this as a gratuitous alienation as it had not been given for adequate consideration, as there was no benefit to that particular company from it. The court held that it was for the creditor to show that the consideration was adequate, and the bank had not succeeded in doing so, and this was therefore a gratuitous alienation: the bank was getting more than normal benefit from the fact that the other three companies were insolvent at the time the transaction was entered into.

In England and Wales there is a similar but distinct challenge of transactions at an undervalue.

(2) *Unfair preferences* under s 243 similarly apply to Scotland only. They are transactions which favour one creditor to the prejudice of the general body of creditors. They are challengeable in court if they were entered into within 6 months prior to the commencement of the winding up. As with the gratuitous alienation, the challenge can be brought by the liquidator, a creditor, or, in the case of a company in administration, an administrator. Examples of an unfair preference might be the granting of a security to a loan that was previously unsecured, or repayment of one creditor ahead of the due date for payment when other creditors are still waiting for payment. In the event of a successful challenge in court, the creditor will remain a creditor, but might have to return money to the liquidator and wait to be paid by the liquidator according to the statutory order of priority. Like the gratuitous alienation, there are exceptions, which, if proved, make the transaction immune from challenge:

(a) transactions in the ordinary course of business;

(b) payments in cash for debts due and payable, unless the transaction was collusive with the purpose of prejudicing the creditors;

(c) transactions in which both parties undertook reciprocal obligations, unless collusive;

(d) the implementation of a mandate from the company allowing funds arrested in the hands of a third party to be paid to the arresting creditor in implement of a court order.

It should be noted that where a company repays a loan or an instalment of a loan at the correct time according to the contract, that would not be an unfair preference just because it takes place in the 6-month period. In such a case, that would be an example of either or both of (a) and (b) above. It would become challengeable if, for example, the repayment was accelerated and made ahead of the due date, or a security was granted to a previously unsecured loan.

In *Anderson* v *Dickens* (2009), a director who had repaid investors within the 6-month period was held liable for an unfair preference, rather than the investors themselves, because he had guaranteed the investment, and the repayment discharged his guarantee.

In *Elmcross Ltd* v *Taylor* (2010), the court held that where a director had obtained an illegal loan from a company, it was repayable either as a gratuitous alienation or an unfair preference, where the director offered none of the defences permitted by ss 242 and 243.

The gratuitous alienation and unfair preference are also available as challenges at common law, which were not abolished when the statutory versions were enacted. Their only advantage is that they do not have time limits attached. They are harder to prove and unlikely to be used.

(3) It is possible for *extortionate credit transactions* to be challenged in court by a liquidator or administrator under s 244 if they took place within the 3 years prior to the commencement of the liquidation. To be challengeable, the terms of the transaction must be proved to involve grossly exorbitant payments, or otherwise grossly contravene ordinary principles of fair dealing. In the event of a successful challenge, the court may set aside the transaction, vary the terms, require repayment to be made to the liquidator, or require surrender to the liquidator of property of the company held in security. Unsurprisingly, the provision has not been much used, as it would be difficult to make a good case in relation to a commercial company that might be expected to have taken financial or legal advice at the time.

(4) Certain *floating charges may become invalid* in consequence of the liquidation, by virtue of s 245. This applies to floating charges created within the 12 months prior to the date of commencement of the liquidation, unless the company can be shown to have been solvent at the time when the charge was created, or new consideration was given for the charge. If the charge was granted to a person connected to the company (a director or shadow director or an associate of the company as defined in s 435), the time period within which the floating charge may be challengeable is extended back 2 years from the commencement of the liquidation, and in this case the solvency at the point when the charge is granted is irrelevant. The charge would only be valid in these circumstances if new consideration was given. It must be emphasised that most floating charges are granted in exchange for

new money granted at the time the charge is given, and their validity is not affected by this provision. The purpose of this section is to try to be fair to the general body of creditors, by preventing people who perhaps hold an unsecured loan, and particularly those who might have inside information about the state of the company's finances, from unfairly taking advantage by obtaining a security in the run-up to the liquidation. The effect of a successful challenge under this section is to make the creditor an unsecured creditor in respect of the claim.

Pursuing the directors and others

Having examined the company's affairs, the liquidator may consider that the directors' conduct in running the company is at fault. It is possible for the directors (and some others) to be made personally liable if various breaches of duty can be proved. Depending on the circumstances, the following provisions may be used:

- There is a summary remedy under s 212 of the Insolvency Act 1986 which can be used where there is evidence that a director or directors have misapplied or retained or become accountable for company money or property, or have breached their fiduciary or other duties as directors. This section gives power to the liquidator, or any creditor or contributory, to apply to the court. The court can order repayment of money or restoration of property to the company, or can order the director to make a contribution to the assets of the company in order to pay the creditors. In *Blin* v *Johnstone* (1988), a company liquidator raised an action under s 212 against one of the former directors, seeking repayment of £6,975, which was the unpaid remainder of a long-term loan. The sheriff ordered the director to repay the loan and on appeal the Inner House held that the important point was that the directors knew that the company was insolvent at the time when the payment was made, not that the payment of the loan brought about the insolvency, and refused the appeal.

- *Fraudulent trading.* Another possible course of action for a liquidator to pursue is an application to court on the ground of fraudulent trading under s 213 of the Insolvency Act 1986. This section provides that a liquidator can apply to the court if in the course of a winding up it appears that "any business of the company has been carried on with intent to defraud creditors or for any fraudulent purpose". The liquidator can use this provision to impose personal liability on any person who was knowingly party to the company's carrying on business in this way, and the court can order the person to contribute to the company's assets to help to pay the creditors to the extent that the court considers appropriate. Usually this provision is used against the directors, but it has been used against creditors who were fully aware of the fact that they received payment from the company obtained by fraudulent trading. In *Re Gerald Cooper Chemicals Ltd* (1978) a creditor received payment of nearly the full amount of the loan out of the deposit paid by a customer for an order of indigo dye for dyeing blue jeans. Lord Templeman remarked in his judgment: "A man who warms himself with the fire of fraud cannot complain if he is singed."

In order to prove a case on this ground, and obtain an order making a party personally liable to contribute to the assets of the company, it is necessary to prove intentional dishonesty, involving real moral blame as shown in *Re Patrick and Lyon Ltd* (1933). This is very hard to do, as it involves proving subjective intention, and of criminal fraud. A case in Scotland in which the directors escaped liability because their acts were in bad faith but not fraudulent was *Rossleigh Ltd* v *Carlaw* (1986). Not surprisingly, there have been relatively few successful cases, as often the issue has not been a deliberate attempt to defraud, but extremely poor book-keeping coupled with a gung-ho attitude to business. To deal with this gap, a further challenge of *wrongful trading* was introduced in the mid-1980s.

Fraudulent trading is also a criminal offence under s 993 of the Companies Act 2006.

- *Wrongful trading.* The liquidator can use s 214 of the Insolvency Act 1986 to challenge acts of the directors and shadow directors in court to seek to make them personally liable to contribute to the assets of the insolvent company. Whereas s 213 can be used in any kind of liquidation, s 213 can only be used if the company is in insolvent liquidation. It has to be proved to the satisfaction of the court that, prior to the winding up, the director knew or ought to have concluded that there was no reasonable prospect of the company's avoiding going into insolvent liquidation, and, when that point was reached, the director did not take all reasonable steps to minimise losses to creditors. Unlike s 213, where fraud has to be proved, s 214 makes use of a two-part statutory standard of care that has since been adopted generally for directors in s 174 of the Companies Act 2006, as discussed in Chapter 8. The director's conduct is measured against (a) the knowledge, skill and experience reasonably to be expected of a person in a similar position to that director and (b) the knowledge, skill and experience of that particular director. This prevents directors escaping liability by pleading lack of knowledge, skill and experience. The first case on this ground was *Re Produce Marketing Consortium Ltd (No 2)* (1989). This provision also extends to shadow directors.

There is a distinct possibility that proceedings brought on the grounds of fraudulent or wrongful trading may be unsuccessful, leaving the company with consequent liability for expenses, putting pressure on the remaining funds to repay creditors. Therefore, since the passage of the Enterprise Act 2002 the liquidator now has to obtain the permission of the creditors or the court before bringing these cases.

Distribution of assets to creditors

Once the liquidator has gathered in all the company's assets, the next step is to pay the creditors in order. The order in which creditors are paid is set out in r 4.66 of the Insolvency (Scotland) Rules 1986. If the company has granted securities, they will interrupt this order, as will be explained. If there is insufficient money to pay any class of creditor in full, the claims abate equally, so that the creditors in that class will receive a dividend of less than £1 per pound, and the next class of creditors below will receive nothing. The order of payment is as follows, in a company that has not granted any securities:

- the expenses of the liquidation, which include the liquidator's fees and expenses;
- in a compulsory liquidation, next come the expenses of any voluntary arrangement if there was one at the time when the petition for winding up was first presented;
- next come the preferential creditors as set out in s 386 of and Sch 6 to the Insolvency Act 1986. These are the same preferential creditors as have a claim in a receivership (discussed in the previous chapter), which nowadays principally consist of claims related to employees' unpaid wages or salary due in the 4 months prior to the commencement of the liquidation, capped at £800 per person, plus related payments;
- next come the claims of ordinary creditors, ie all those creditors who do not hold securities or have any other preference. They would include suppliers of goods on credit, customers who have paid deposits for goods or services that they have not received,

utility companies, and the government for various taxes including pay as you earn income tax, value added tax and corporation tax, plus local authority business rates, some but not all of which were preferential until the passage of the Enterprise Act 2002, but are no longer;

• after the ordinary creditors, interest is paid on the preferential debts and the ordinary debts;

• finally, postponed debts are paid. The Insolvency (Scotland) Rules 1986 state that these are the claims of creditors who have had a gratuitous alienation reduced. However, by s 735 of the Companies Act 2006 (as was seen in Chapter 10), if the company does not perform its contract to purchase or redeem its own shares, the affected shareholder is a postponed creditor, who will be paid before any return of surplus to members.

As mentioned above, there may be creditors who hold securities. Under these Rules, a creditor with a fixed security such as a standard security over land or buildings belonging to the company has the right to sell the asset without reference to the liquidator, repay himself out of the proceeds, and return any surplus to the liquidator. Alternatively, the liquidator can pay the secured creditor the value of the fixed security in full and then sell the asset to provide funds for the other creditors.

In the case of a creditor who holds a floating charge, the position is that under s 175 of the Insolvency Act 1986, preferential creditors have preference over the claim of the floating charge creditor. As was discussed in Chapter 14 in relation to receivership, and also in Chapter 13 on creditors, since the passage of the Enterprise Act 2002, provision has to be made for retention of some money for the ordinary creditors before paying the floating charge creditor (the "prescribed part"). So, if there is a floating charge, the floating charge creditor would be paid after the preferential creditors, but under deduction of the prescribed part.

In the case of the liquidation of a solvent company, after paying all the creditors, there may be a surplus remaining to be returned to the members. This will be done as with any return of capital, according to the members' rights. It is to be remembered that a company may have been put into voluntary liquidation because it is no longer needed, or, as seen in Chapter 11, it may have been put into compulsory liquidation on the just and equitable ground by a member or members in extreme situations when there is no other remedy and the members have lost all confidence in the company's management.

Completion of the liquidation

When all payments to creditors (and, where appropriate, members) have been made, final accounts will be prepared by the liquidator. In a compulsory liquidation, a final meeting of creditors will be convened, while in a members' voluntary liquidation there will be a meeting of members and in a creditors' voluntary liquidation meetings of both members and creditors under ss 146, 94 and 106 respectively. Notice is given to the court in the case of a compulsory liquidation and also to Companies House; and, in the case of voluntary liquidation, to Companies House. This is registered and 3 months later the company is dissolved, which means that its name is taken off the Register and it ceases to be a legal person.

Restoration of a company to the Register

Once a company has been removed from the Register, it is possible for it to be restored to the Register again for certain purposes. This might be because an employee has contracted an industrial disease through exposure to harmful substances in the course of working for the company (eg asbestos workers, who may contract asbestosis), and an industrial disease often manifests itself many years after the time when the harm was done. The company should have insurance which continues to provide cover. A former director or former member may apply to the Registrar of Companies for the restoration of the company to the Register under s 1024 of the Companies Act 2006, subject to a 6-year time limit. In other cases there has to be an application to the court under ss 1029–1030 of the Companies Act 2006. In the case of a claim based on personal injuries there is no time limit.

Sometimes companies are removed from the Register because they have failed to file annual accounts or annual returns at Companies House, under s 1000 of the Companies Act 2006. The directors will have received a series of warning letters, which they will have ignored. In such a case, if the company is in fact in operation, it can be restored to the Register on application by the directors under s 1024 within the time limit. If a company is dissolved and has assets, these assets are classed as *bona vacantia* (ownerless goods) which are deemed to belong to the Crown if the directors do nothing to have the company restored to the Register.

DISSOLUTION WITHOUT LIQUIDATION

Most companies that come to the end of their useful life do not go through liquidation, but instead are just dissolved. It is only useful to put a company into liquidation if there are some unpaid creditors, and if there are some funds with which to pay creditors. In a hopelessly insolvent company where there is not even money to meet the liquidator's fees, liquidation is impractical. Likewise, a solvent company that is no longer needed, and where there is a small number of members, may be able to pay all its creditors and sort out the return of capital to members without needing to go through liquidation. In these cases, once its affairs have been sorted out, the directors of the company can apply to Companies House to have it struck off on the ground that it is not carrying on business or in operation under s 1003 of the Companies Act 2006. A company that has completed an administration may also be dissolved without liquidation if it wishes, again by notification to Companies House, under para 84 of Sch B1 to the Insolvency Act 1986, if the company has no property at that point.

Essential Facts

- When a company goes into liquidation, its affairs are brought to a close and it will eventually cease to exist as a legal person. A liquidator is in charge.
- A liquidation can be voluntary (initiated by the members) or compulsory (ordered by the court).
- A voluntary liquidation can be a members' voluntary liquidation or a creditors' voluntary liquidation.
- Steps may be taken to find various parties liable to contribute to the assets of the company because of things done prior to the commencement of the liquidation.
- In a liquidation, creditors are paid in a set order of priority.
- In some cases companies can be dissolved without liquidation.

Essential Cases

Jackson v Royal Bank of Scotland (2002): an inter-company guarantee arrangement covering overdraft facilities to connected companies could be a gratuitous alienation if all but one of the companies were insolvent at the time of the arrangement as the guarantee in these circumstances gave the bank more than would usually be the case. It was for the bank to prove that the consideration was adequate and it had not done so.

Anderson v Dickens (2009): in some circumstances a director might be liable on an unfair preference, where repaying investors indirectly benefited the director who had guaranteed the investment.

Elmcross Ltd v Taylor (2010): an illegal loan received within the 6-month time limit prior to the commencement of a liquidation could be repayable either as a gratuitous alienation or an unfair preference where the director did not offer any of the statutory defences.

Re Gerald Cooper Chemicals Ltd (1978): a creditor could be personally liable for fraudulent trading where repayment of a loan was accepted in circumstances where the lender knew that the money came from deposits from customers who would not get paid.

Re Patrick and Lyon Ltd (1933): to establish liability for fraudulent trading under s 213 of the Insolvency Act 1986, proof of intentional dishonesty, involving real moral blame, is required.

Rossleigh Ltd v Carlaw (1986): where the directors of a company breached the terms of its lease and transferred all its assets to another company and ceased to trade without informing the landlord, a case brought against the directors for fraudulent trading failed on the ground that the directors had acted in bad faith but not fraudulently, and it was held that fraud in the criminal sense needed to be proved.

Re Produce Marketing Consortium Ltd (No 2) (1989): where the directors of a company had had it pointed out to them by the auditor that the company was insolvent and their response was to reduce liability to one creditor by increasing liability to another, the directors were held to be personally liable for wrongful trading in the eventual insolvent liquidation of the company. They should have known that the liabilities were greater than the assets and were found not to have taken steps to minimise losses to the creditors.

16 COMPANY RECONSTRUCTION

Companies need to adapt to changing circumstances if they are to succeed in business. As has been seen elsewhere in this book, small private companies may grow and be re-registered as public companies, and they may eventually have their securities listed on the London Stock Exchange. Similarly, companies may encounter economic problems and there may be a need to restructure the company or group of companies. It may also be that one company buys the shares or a majority of the shares of another, so that the other company becomes its subsidiary. The reasoning behind these structural changes is economic: a company that makes a takeover bid for the shares of another company thinks that it can make a profit from the company it purchases. Another possibility is that two companies are merged to become one. The purpose of this chapter is to explore all these different procedures.

SCHEMES OF ARRANGEMENT

Schemes of arrangement allow a company to make a compromise or arrangement with its members or creditors. This might be used in order to reconstruct the company's share capital or loan capital and it might be used in relation to a whole group of companies. The scheme of arrangement is very versatile and can also be used as a method of uncontested takeover of the shares in a target company instead of a takeover bid (the shareholders of the target company will instead be given shares in the offeror company in exchange for their existing shares). It might be used with creditors, perhaps to swap debt for equity. It is also extensively used where insurance companies are going out of business. Shareholders' rights and creditors' rights are likely to be changed by this process, and one of the requirements of the procedure is that there must be some degree of compromise on the part of the participants. The procedure is found in ss 895–901 of the Companies Act 2006. It is a complicated procedure that requires the involvement of the court, which makes the procedure lengthy, commonly taking about 8 weeks, and it is consequently more suited to larger companies.

An application is made to the court by the company itself, a member, creditor, the liquidator (if the company is in liquidation) or the administrator (if the company is in administration) asking the court to order meetings of the members or separate classes of members, or of creditors or separate classes of creditors as appropriate to the particular company, to consider the proposed scheme of arrangement. Separate meetings will be organised for groups with divergent interests. The participants must receive full information of the proposed scheme with the notice of the meeting.

The required majority of creditors and of members, and each separate class of them, is a majority in number and 75 per cent in value, under s 899. If these thresholds are met, the court may approve the scheme. However, the court will not approve a scheme of arrangement unless it is a genuine compromise, and the court's role is to see fair play among the various interest groups, as shown in *Re NFU Development Trust Ltd* (1973) in which a scheme whereby most members gave up their rights was held not to be a genuine compromise. In *Re Hellenic and General Trust Ltd* (1975) the court held that a company that held 53 per cent of the shares of Hellenic and which was the subsidiary of a company that the scheme of arrangement proposed would acquire Hellenic, should not have been at the same meeting as other ordinary shareholders, as their interests were not the same.

Where the scheme is to be used to effect a reconstruction or amalgamation, and assets are to be transferred from one company to another, the court has various powers under s 900: these include power to order the transfer of assets, power to order the allotment or appropriation of shares or debentures, power to order the dissolution of the transferor company without winding up, and power to make provision for dissentient members or creditors.

Once a scheme is sanctioned by the court, it is binding on all the members and creditors, even if they did not vote for it, and it must be implemented.

TAKEOVERS

A takeover involves an offeror company making an offer to the shareholders of a target company to buy their shares. If the shareholders of the target company like the terms of the offer, they will sell their shares. If the offeror company is able to acquire sufficient shares in the target company it will become a subsidiary or a wholly owned subsidiary of the offeror company as defined in s 1159. The making of a bid and the acceptance (or not) by shareholders is a contractual matter. The directors of the target company will inform the shareholders of the boards' view of the bid, and in doing so they must act in conformity to their duties as directors (discussed in Chapter 8). If the directors do not think that the bid is good for the company or its shareholders, it is a hostile bid.

In companies that are not listed on the London Stock Exchange, a takeover may be agreed between an offeror and the members and directors of the target company, following which a sale and purchase agreement will be drawn up for the purchase either of the assets of the company or of its shares. If the assets are purchased, the target company will eventually be wound up. If all the shares in the target company are bought, it will become a wholly owned subsidiary of the offeror as defined in s 1159(2) of the Companies Act 2006.

Takeovers are largely a matter of the law of contract. However, the EC Takeovers Directive 2004/25/EC has brought about some changes to the law to provide a statutory framework for the body that regulates takeovers, to provide some rights when there is a minority of 10 per cent or fewer left after a takeover bid has been made, and to restrict the ability to throw up barriers to takeovers.

The Panel on Takeovers and Mergers

This body used to be a non-statutory body, but is now statutory under rules in ss 942–965 of the Companies Act 2006, following the Takeovers Directive. The Panel is made up of up to 35 members drawn from the bodies whose members work in the field of takeovers and mergers, such as the British Bankers Association and the Confederation of British Industry. The Panel regulates the conduct of takeover bids, mergers and other inter-company arrangements and has power to make rules. More information about the Panel on Takeovers and Mergers is to be found on its website: www.thetakeoverpanel.org.uk.

The rules are found in the Takeover Code, which now has statutory force. The Takeover Code is a distillation of the collective opinion of professionals about appropriate business standards that should apply during a bid. It provides six general principles relating to fairness to all holders of securities in an offeree company; it imposes a duty on the directors of the offeree company to act in the interests of the company as a whole and to give their members an opportunity to decide for themselves on the merits of the bid; there is a prohibition on the creation of false markets in the shares of either the offeror or offeree companies; there is a requirement that an offeror who makes a bid must be able to follow through with a cash offer; and there is a requirement that the offeree company should not be hindered in the conduct of its affairs by the bid longer than is reasonable. There is a rule in the Takeover Code that once an offeror acquires a 30 per cent holding, it must make a mandatory bid for the remainder. This is because a 30 per cent holding would allow it to block a special resolution and would generally give it *de facto* control of the target. Until a bid has been made, the Takeover Code demands that absolute secrecy must be maintained until the bid is announced and there are restrictions on dealing in the shares of both companies before and during the bid to prevent insider dealing.

The Panel gives guidance on the interpretation of the Takeover Code, and enforces compliance. It has disciplinary powers over professionals who work on bids. Where the rules have been breached, it can give private or public censure and can demand that compensation for breach of the rules be paid. It may also apply to a court for an order for enforcement of the rules under s 955. It can report financial services professionals to the Financial Services Authority for disciplinary action to be taken in respect market misconduct or other of breach of the rules, and other professionals can be reported to their own supervisory bodies in cases of breach.

Regulation of takeovers under ss 942–992 of the Companies Act 2006

Where a takeover bidder has acquired 90 per cent or more of the target company's shares which are the subject of an offer, the holders of the remaining 10 per cent shares are powerless to do very much, as they cannot prevent any ordinary or special resolutions being passed. To counter this, there are provisions allowing the offeror to make a compulsory purchase for the rest ("squeeze out") and for the minority to force a purchase of their remaining shares ("sell out").

Squeeze out

By ss 974–982, when a bidder reaches 90 per cent of the target company's shares to which the offer relates, it can compel the remaining 10 per cent shareholders to sell their shares to it. To have this power, the offer must have been to acquire all of the target company's shares or all the shares of a particular class. The holding of the offeror in each class must be 90 per cent in value and 90 per cent by voting rights. The offeror must given notice within 3 months of achieving the 90 per cent threshold to the holders of the remaining 10 per cent that it intends to compel the sale of the remaining shares. The terms of the compulsory purchase must be the same as the original offer.

Under these rules, a minority shareholder who does not wish to sell his shares can apply to the court within 6 weeks under s 986. The court has power to prohibit the purchase or to vary its terms. However, considering that other shareholders have been happy to sell their shares, the court would only prevent the acquisition or amend the terms in unusual circumstances, such as those in *Re Bugle Press Ltd* (1960) where an offer for all the shares in a company was found not to be a genuine transaction, but a device to expel a minority shareholder, and the court refused to allow the compulsory purchase of the minority's shares.

Sell out

By ss 983–985, when a bidder reaches 90 per cent of all the target company's shares by value and by voting rights (note this is not quite the same as for squeeze out, where the rights apply where the bidder has acquired 90 per cent of the shares which are subject to the bid), the bidder must notify the remaining shareholders within 1 month if it does not intend to purchase the remainder, and must inform the remaining shareholders of their right to be bought out on the same terms as in the bid , or such other terms as may be agreed. The remaining shareholders can insist on being bought out on the terms of the offer by making a written request within 3 months.

Rules to prevent frustration of a takeover bid

Companies might wish to frustrate a takeover bid by such devices as attaching special voting rights to shares or by imposing restrictions on the right to transfer shares or requiring shares to be transferred. The EC Takeovers Directive attempted to restrict both pre-bid and post-bid defensive tactics but, due to differing views in different Member States, the Directive was a compromise and Member States were permitted to choose different legislative options. The UK has chosen not to restrict the use of pre-bid defences by mandatory law, but has allowed listed public companies themselves to choose to opt in by special resolution before they can use defensive measures and they can also opt out by a further special resolution. These rules are found in ss 966–973. These relate to listed companies only, which have opted in by special resolution to apply them, which they can do only if they do not have restrictions written into their Articles of Association.

Where the company has opted in, breakthrough rights apply, and the rule is that, once a bid has been made, any restrictions attaching to shares will not apply to voting on defensive measures to frustrate a bid. Likewise, agreements which place restrictions on transfers of shares to the offeror during the offer period, or to any other person once the offeror has achieved 75 per cent or more of the voting shares, would not apply.

Also, if, after the bid, the offeror holds 75 per cent or more of the shares carrying voting rights, at the first meeting after the end of the offer period, all shares will have one vote each, and transfer restrictions or voting restrictions will not apply.

In an opted-in company, an offeror who has acquired 75 per cent or more of the voting shares in the target company can requisition a general meeting in accordance with ss 303–305 of the Companies Act 2006, under s 969 of the Act.

The UK has made these optional, ie the usual rule is that these do *not* apply in the UK unless a company specifically opts in by special resolution (it can opt out again by another special resolution). Other Member States have applied them fully. In the UK, companies' Articles have tended to present very few barriers to takeovers, as the merits of having a vigorous market in takeovers has been recognised by the business community in the UK.

MERGERS

In a merger or amalgamation, two or more companies become one. This effect could be achieved in various ways: there could be a transfer of assets from Company A to Company B followed by the liquidation of Company A; or a scheme of arrangement under ss 895–901 could be used, as discussed earlier in this chapter.

One very specialised method of effecting a merger between Company A and Company B is under rules in s 110 of the Insolvency Act 1986. This section provides for Company A to enter voluntary liquidation, whereupon if it is put into members' voluntary liquidation it can pass a special resolution authorising the liquidator to transfer its assets to Company B, usually in exchange for shares in Company B, which will then be distributed to the shareholders of Company A. Company A will then be wound up. A company which is in creditors' voluntary liquidation can make the same arrangement with the consent of the court or the liquidation committee rather than by passing a special resolution.

Such a sale is then binding on the members of Company A. However, where the authority for this form of merger comes in the form of a special resolution, s 111 of the Insolvency Act 1986 allows any dissentient member to give written notice within 7 days demanding that the liquidator either abandon the scheme or buy out the dissentient member's shares before the company is dissolved. This mechanism could be used to effect a merger of two or more companies into one, or a demerger of one company into more than one. It is attractive in that it does not need to involve the court, unlike the scheme of arrangement. However, its less attractive quality is that it is useful only where there is no dissent, as a member with a large holding who is insisting on being bought out could make the scheme uneconomic; and, consequently, it is not widely used in practice.

The European company

The European company or *societas Europaea* (SE) is a business vehicle that can facilitate mergers. This special form of company has its own European regulation (Regulation 2157/2001 on the Statute for a European Company). A *societas Europaea* can be formed either by the merger of two existing SEs, or where two SEs create a joint parent or joint subsidiary. The purpose of this business vehicle is to facilitate cross-border mergers. To date, they have not been widely used in the UK.

ISSUES OF COMPETITION LAW WITH TAKEOVERS AND MERGERS

In some cases a proposed takeover of another company or merger of two companies into one may restrict consumer choice and may therefore potentially distort the market. A proposed takeover or merger may be referred to the Competition Commission by the Office of Fair Trading. The Competition Commission has the power under the Enterprise Act 2002 to decide whether the takeover or merger can go ahead. If a merger has a "community dimension" because of the size and scale of the company to be created by the merger, as expressed in its combined world-wide turnover, it may become a matter for adjudication by the European Commission rather than the Competition Commission by virtue of the EC Merger Regulation (Council Regulation (EC) 139/2004).

Essential Facts

- The structure of companies may have to change in response to changing economic circumstances. A company may wish to reconstruct its share or loan capital structure; one company may wish to take over another by purchasing its shares; two or more companies may wish to merge to become one.

- A **scheme of arrangement** under ss 895–901 of the Companies Act 2006 may be used to carry out a wide range of changes such as the reconstruction of share capital or loan capital of a company or the merger of two companies. A scheme of arrangement needs the approval of the court.

- A **takeover** by share purchase by Company A of the shares of Company B is a contractual matter. However, a statutory body, the Panel on Takeovers and Mergers, oversees takeovers and mergers; and some statutory rules ensure that small, powerless minorities do not remain after a takeover if either the minority or the bidder does not so wish. There are also some statutory rules to prevent frustration of a takeover bid.

- In a **merger** two or more companies will become one. The scheme of arrangement could be used to effect a merger. Another method is an arrangement under s 110 of the Insolvency Act 1986 which involves putting one company into voluntary liquidation and transferring all its assets to another company, following which the shareholders of the first company usually receive shares in the second company. Where the company is insolvent, the consent of the liquidation committee or the court must be obtained, to protect the creditors. And any one dissentient member can kill the scheme by demanding that he is bought out by the liquidator before the scheme goes ahead.

- The European company is a vehicle that can be used to facilitate a merger, particularly a cross-border merger between companies based in more than one Member State of the European Union.

- Where a proposed takeover or merger is between very large companies, there are potential effects on free competition and possible harm could be done to consumers' interests. Such mergers may be referred by the Office of Fair Trading to the Competition Commission, and in cases where there is a "Community dimension" the European Commission may consider the proposed merger.

Essential Cases

Re NFU Development Trust Ltd (1973): in a scheme of arrangement under ss 895–901 of the Companies Act 2006 there must be a true compromise involving some give and take on both sides: in this case it was proposed that the membership of the company be reduced from 98,000 voting members to seven. Despite an 85 per cent vote in favour, the court refused to sanction the scheme of arrangement because it was not a compromise.

Re Hellenic and General Trust Ltd (1975): where a majority shareholder had different interests from those of the minority, the court refused to sanction a scheme of arrangement on the ground that the rest of the ordinary shareholders should have had a separate meeting to consider and approve the scheme.

Re Bugle Press Ltd (1960): a bidder for shares who has achieved a 90 per cent holding usually has the right to acquire the remainder, although a minority may be able to prevent this by applying to court. Although usually this application would probably be unsuccessful, as most other shareholders have already agreed to sell their shares, in this case the court held that the takeover bid was a sham with the purpose of trying to expel the minority shareholder.

17 INSIDER DEALING AND MARKET ABUSE

Insider dealing and market abuse are closely related and overlapping concepts. Market abuse is a more generic concept that includes insider dealing. They exist in parallel because the law relating to these concepts developed separately, with insider dealing having a longer history.

Insider dealing takes place when a person is in possession of confidential price-sensitive information which he should keep confidential: instead, he makes use of that information to buy or sell securities on a regulated market hoping to make a profit or avoid a loss. If the information is a positive story about the company, the person stands to make a profit, whereas if it is bad news, the person stands to avoid a loss, because the share price at the time when the deal is made is not the correct one, since the news is not known to the market generally. Giving a hot tip to someone else can also be insider dealing. Often insider dealing takes place when one company is planning to make a takeover bid for another company and that fact is still supposed to be confidential under the Takeover Code.

Market abuse is a much wider concept that covers insider dealing but also includes various other ways in which markets can be manipulated to create a false market in securities: for example, ramping schemes, in which securities are "talked up", and schemes to deceive the market about securities.

Insider dealing and market abuse are harmful to the market because people have to believe that the market is fair and not rigged in favour of those "in the know". If that cynical view of the market were widespread, people just would not bother investing in it and would look for a cleaner market. Therefore there needs to be an effective enforcement regime to eliminate insider dealing and market abuse if the market is to prosper. The enforcement regime will be discussed later in this chapter.

These activities are controlled in various ways under different statutes: some activities attract criminal penalties, while others attract civil penalties (with some overlap, giving scope for choice of regime by the enforcers) and there are some other legal consequences that may apply in specific circumstances.

Much of the law comes from the European Union Directive on Insider Dealing and Market Manipulation 2003/6/EC.

The law on insider dealing and market abuse applies to the whole of the United Kingdom, including Scotland and Northern Ireland.

This area of law is the responsibility of HM Treasury in the UK. Currently, the regulator is the Financial Services Authority (www.fsa. gov.uk), which acts as the UK Listing Authority in relation to the listing of securities on the public markets in the UK. It also regulates financial institutions, and, as will be seen in this chapter, enforces the law on insider dealing and market abuse. It has another function of consumer protection in relation to financial services. The government has proposals to replace this body with a new independent financial regulator, the Consumer Protection and Markets Authority, by 2012 or possibly 2013. The new body will continue to carry on the function of UK Listing Authority, and will continue to regulate how firms in the financial services sector conduct business, exercising criminal and administrative enforcement powers over market conduct. Its consumer protection function will also continue. Some of the current functions of the Financial Services Authority in relation to financial institutions would be passed to a new Prudential Regulation Authority, which will be a subsidiary of the Bank of England.

This chapter will first explore the older criminal law that applies to insider dealing. This will be following by a discussion of the criminal law and civil penalties regime that applies to market abuse. The final section will deal with various other civil consequences that may arise.

INSIDER DEALING

Criminal Justice Act 1993

Insider dealing is regulated by the criminal law in Pt V (ss 52–64) of the Criminal Justice Act 1993, which apply to Scotland and Northern Ireland as well as to England and Wales. Section 52 makes it a criminal offence for an individual (not a company) to deal in price-affected securities on a regulated market in the UK on the basis of inside information which the individual knows to be inside information and which he knows to have come from an inside source. It is also a criminal offence to encourage another person to deal, whether or not the other person knows the securities are price-affected, and disclosing such information otherwise than in the proper performance of his duties is also a criminal offence. The accused must be within the UK when the insider dealing is alleged to have taken place (s 62). This offence involves proof of *mens rea* (or intention) on the part of the accused, and it must be proved beyond reasonable doubt that the person knows the information is confidential and that he knows it comes from an inside source.

There are various defences that might be used. It is a defence to prove that the individual did not expect at the time the dealing was done that it would result in a profit to follow from the fact that the information was price-sensitive. Another defence is to show that the individual believed at the time of the dealing reasonable grounds that the information was in the public domain, and by s 58 it is clear that, provided it is published in accordance with the rules of the regulated market, to be in the public domain the information does not need to be readily available to everyone, but may have been drawn to the attention of only a section of the public. A third defence is to show that the individual would have done what he did anyway even if he did not have the confidential information: this might perhaps be a good defence if a person has to realise an asset for financial reasons and these securities are his one liquid asset. There is a defence to a charge of encouraging another person to deal to show that he did not expect the dealing to result in a profit attributable to the fact that the information was price-sensitive or that at the time he believed on reasonable grounds that the information had been sufficiently disseminated to the public, or that he would have done what he did anyway even without the confidential information. There is a defence to a charge of disclosing confidential price-sensitive information, to show that the individual did not expect any person to deal on the basis of the disclosure, or that although he did expect the person to deal at the time, he did not expect the dealing to result in a profit attributable to the fact that the information was price-sensitive information in relation to securities. There are special defences in Sch 1 for professional market makers.

Insider dealing can be tried either summarily or on indictment (with a jury). On indictment, a 7-year jail sentence and/or an unlimited fine may be used. In a summary trial, the maximum sentence is imprisonment for up to 6 months or a fine of the statutory maximum. Confiscation orders may also be used.

It has proved difficult to secure convictions for insider dealing because of the need to prove the *mens rea* (criminal intention) necessary to this offence, and to establish this to the criminal standard of proof beyond reasonable doubt. In Scotland, corroboration by at least two pieces of evidence is needed. Often the only evidence is the deal itself or the word of one other person, where it becomes an issue of which of the parties is to be believed. In *Mackie v HM Advocate* (1994) an investment analyst successfully appealed against conviction for insider dealing in Scotland on the grounds that there was insufficient corroboration and the fact that the dealing took place was held to be a neutral rather than an incriminating event.

However, there have been some notable recent convictions, one being *R v Butt* (2006) in which the vice-president of an investment bank Credit Suisse First Boston, who worked in the section of the bank concerned with the secrecy of dealings, was jailed for 5 years (reduced to 4 years on appeal), having used confidential price-sensitive information on numerous occasions to do spread betting on the movements of companies' shares before public announcements were made. Recently, a successful prosecution for insider dealing was brought against Christian Littlewood, a senior investment banker, his wife Angie Littlewood and another person to whom tips were given, who carried out the insider dealing for the three of them. Littlewood was sentenced to 3 years and 4 months in 2011, his wife to 12 months' suspended sentence and the third person was given 2 years and ordered to repay £640,000.

MARKET ABUSE

Financial Services and Markets Act 2000 (FSMA 2000)

This important statute does many things, one of them being to create the main regulatory body in the field: the Financial Services Authority (s 1). The Financial Services Authority is the Listing Authority in relation to listing of securities on the London Stock Exchange and various other regulated markets in the UK. It also authorises people to carry out various regulated activities, such as stockbrokers, investment managers, financial advisers and insurers. It also has powers to investigate market abuse under s 168 and can both prosecute market abuse and pursue civil penalties under the two regimes created by this Act.

Criminal law regime

Two subsections of s 397 of FSMA 2000 create two criminal offences. Unlike the offences under the Criminal Justice Act 1993, these can apply to companies and their directors as well as to individuals. The offences relate to securities traded on a public market.

Under s 397(1) and (2) it is an offence for a person to make a statement which he knows to be misleading, dishonestly to conceal facts, or recklessly to make a statement, for the purpose of inducing another person to enter into an agreement relating to securities. To convict a person of this offence needs proof of *mens rea*. There are certain defences available to professional market makers. In *R* v *Rigby* (2006), Rigby and a fellow company director were successfully prosecuted under s 397(1) for market abuse for operating a share ramping scheme and Rigby was disqualified from acting as a director for 6 years under provisions in the Company Directors Disqualification Act 1986.

The other criminal offence under this statute is s 397(3), which makes it an offence to do an act or engage in conduct that creates a false or misleading impression as to the market, if the act is done for the purpose of creating that impression, and of inducing another person to invest in or dispose of securities or to refrain from doing so. In contrast to s 397(1), this offence does not need proof of *mens rea*, although some degree of intention would have to be proved. It is a defence to the offence under s 397(3) to prove that the person believed on reasonable grounds that the act or conduct would not create a false or misleading impression of the market, and various more technical defences for market makers apply to both subsections.

These offences are triable either summarily or on indictment and the penalties are the same as for insider dealing under the Criminal Justice Act 1993 (s 398(8)).

In Scotland, prosecutions are in the hands of the Crown Office. In England and Wales, prosecutions can be brought by the Financial Services Authority as well as with the consent of the Director of Public Prosecutions. A similar rule applies to Northern Ireland.

Regime of administrative penalties

Prosecutions under the Criminal Justice Act 1993 and s 397 of the Financial Services and Markets Act 2000 and their predecessors have not been very successful because of the need to prove *mens rea* and to reach the criminal standard of proof. For that reason, a regime providing for administrative penalties for market abuse was introduced by ss 118–121 of the Financial Services and Markets Act 2000. Section 118 sets out various types of behaviour that can constitute market abuse. The Financial Services and Markets Authority issues a Code that provides guidance on what does and does not constitute market abuse. The Authority can investigate allegations of market abuse and, if it finds evidence, it can issue a warning notice under s 126, warning of its intention to impose a penalty. It then issues a decision notice under s 127. It has the power to impose civil penalties under s 123 of such an amount as the Financial Services Authority considers appropriate. If the person who has received a decision notice wishes to contest it, it can refer the matter to the Financial Services and Markets Tribunal, which is an independent tribunal. The Authority can also apply to the court under s 383 for a restitution order seeking disgorgement of the profits from the market abuse, and the Financial Services Authority can then pay the proceeds to a person to whom the proceeds may be attributable, if any. It may also apply to a court for an interdict in cases where market abuse is likely to occur in order to restrain it in future. Instead of imposing penalties, the Financial Services Authority may censure the person and publicise the fact under s 123. It can also discipline those professionals that are regulated by it, such as stockbrokers, which might involve barring infringers from operating in financial services in future. It can also pass information to other regulatory bodies in cases of market abuse on the part of other professionals. By the Financial Services Act 2010, additional powers have been granted to the Financial Services Authority to suspend authorised persons, to impose restrictions on them and to withdraw their authority.

The types of behaviour that might attract administrative penalties have been changed quite a bit since the Financial Services and Markets Act 2000 was enacted, and are now (s 118) as follows:

- dealing or attempting to deal in a qualifying investment on the basis of inside information;
- disclosing inside information to another person other than in the proper performance of a person's duties (insider dealing);
- effecting transactions or orders to trade for other than legitimate reasons which are likely to give a false or misleading impression as to the supply or demand for or the price of a qualifying investment or which fix the price of a qualifying investment at an artificial level;
- effecting transactions or orders to trade which employ fictitious devices or any other form of deception;
- disseminating information by any means which gives, or is likely to give, a false or misleading impression of a qualifying investment by a person who knew or would reasonably be expected to have known that the information was false or misleading.

At the time of writing, there are some further types of behaviour that attract administrative penalties but these will cease to have effect on 31 December 2011.

Encouraging others to do any of these acts can also be market abuse. By s 123, administrative penalties will not be imposed if the person is able to show in response to a warning notice that he believed on reasonable grounds that his behaviour does not amount to market abuse under s 118 or that he took all reasonable precautions and exercised all due diligence to avoid committing market abuse.

There was some concern when the Financial Services and Markets Bill was being enacted, as to whether these penalties were civil or criminal. In criminal procedure, a greater degree of protection is afforded under Art 6 of the European Convention for the Protection of Human Rights and Fundamental Freedoms than in civil procedure, and the standard of proof is beyond reasonable doubt. Changes were made to the Bill and s 174 makes clear that, in investigations for market abuse, statements made by a person who is under investigation for market abuse are only admissible in court if put forward by the person who was investigated and cannot be used against that person. This is to comply with the presumption of innocence until proven guilty that applies in criminal cases. Also, there is a legal assistance scheme funded by the Financial Services Authority to ensure compliance with Art 6. The Financial Services and Markets Tribunal has viewed the standard of proof required as being proportionate to the seriousness of the allegations, so that more serious cases need a higher standard of proof, as shown in the case of *Davidson and Tatham* v *FSA* (2006). This has made it more difficult for the Financial Services Authority to win cases which are taken by the affected party to the Tribunal, and the Authority lost the Davidson and Tatham cases, with the Tribunal awarding costs against the Authority.

The administrative penalties regime has been used fairly successfully by the Financial Services Authority after a slow start. In 2006, Philippe Jabre, who was a former managing director of a firm that acted as a hedge fund manager, and the firm itself were both fined £750,000 for market abuse in connection with short selling shares in Sumitomo Mitsui based on inside information. In 2010, the largest penalty imposed by the Financial Services Authority so far was imposed on Simon Eagle, a stockbroker, who carried out a share ramping scheme involving a company whose shares were traded on the Alternative Investment Market. The shares had to be suspended from the AIM because of this. Eagle was fined £1.5 million as a penalty, with a £1.3 million order for disgorgement of profit plus a prohibition order against performing any regulated activity.

INVESTIGATIONS INTO INSIDER DEALING AND MARKET ABUSE

Suspicious movements in share prices are picked up by monitoring programmes run by the London Stock Exchange and may be passed to the Financial Services Authority for further investigation. The Financial Services Authority uses a sophisticated IT system called Sabre II to monitor patterns of dealing. Suspicious transactions can be reported to the Financial Services Authority, which has a market abuse reporting hotline. The Financial Services Authority and the government both have power under ss 167–168 of the Financial Services and Markets Act 2000 to investigate both insider dealing under the Criminal Justice Act 1993 and market abuse under the Financial Services and Markets Act 2000. Investigators have power to compel attendance and the production of documents. Statements made to investigators are admissible as evidence in court, but, as stated earlier, an accused person in a criminal court cannot have his own statements made to investigators used in evidence against him (s 174).

DISCLOSURE

The best way to inoculate a market against insider dealing and market abuse is by compulsory disclosure so that the scope for people to have access to price-sensitive information for any length of time is greatly reduced. The Financial Services Authority as the UK Listing Authority has issued Disclosure Rules and Transparency Rules which demand notification of any inside information to a regulatory information service as soon as possible, and publication on the company's website by the end of the next business day. These rules also force public companies whose securities are traded on a regulated market to draw up lists of insiders which must be made available to the Financial Services Authority on request.

These rules also place dealing restrictions on employees who have access to confidential price-sensitive information in the course of their work.

THE NEW "GET TOUGH" APPROACH OF THE FINANCIAL SERVICES AUTHORITY

The recent downturn in the UK economy has put considerable focus on to the behaviour of financial institutions, and questions have been asked about the effectiveness of the regulatory authorities. Possibly as a consequence, there are signs of a new tougher approach by the Financial Services Authority to fight financial crime in regulated firms. After some years of preferring to use the administrative penalties regime, it has recently been making use of its power to prosecute the criminal offences in England and Wales and Northern Ireland (though it does not have this power in Scotland). The Authority has articulated a view that people fear a criminal conviction more than a civil penalty, and it has started to make more use of the criminal regimes under the Criminal Justice Act 1993 and s 397 of the Financial Services and Markets Act 2000. In addition to some recent cases, some of which have been noted in this chapter, at the time of writing there are apparently 12 further insider dealing cases currently under investigation. However, the impending demise of the Financial Services Authority may cause some disruption to this.

OTHER POSSIBLE CONSEQUENCES OF INSIDER DEALING AND MARKET ABUSE

In some circumstances, where a person passes on a tip concerning an investment and the person was given the knowledge in confidence, there may be grounds for an action for breach of confidence, which is a delict. In those areas of work where employees are regularly exposed to confidential information, such as employees of investment banks and those who work in share registration, their contracts of employment are likely to include provisions enforcing a duty to maintain confidentiality of information. In such cases, employees who disclose information other than for the performance of their duties would face dismissal, as well as a possible action for damages. The same would apply to directors.

Directors who engage in market abuse which has repercussions for their company must consider their general duties towards their company, and particularly the duty to promote the success of the company for the benefit of the members as a whole (s 172 of the Companies Act 2006) and the duty not to allow a conflict of interest to arise between the director's duty to the company and the director's own personal interest (s 175). These were considered in Chapter 8.

Directors may also be disqualified from office following conviction for an indictable offence relating to the management of a company under s 2 of the Company Directors Disqualification Act 1986. This happened to Carl Rigby, as mentioned earlier in this chapter (see Essential Cases below).

Despite a view by some that insider dealing is a victimless crime, both it and market abuse can have consequences which have definite victims. In *Chase Manhattan Equities Ltd v Goodman* (1991), Chase Manhattan was very much a loser as a result of Goodman's actions, and in that case a contract tainted by insider dealing was held to be unenforceable.

Essential Facts

- Insider dealing is a type of market abuse: it consists of making use of confidential price-sensitive information which an individual knows is inside information and which he knows came from an inside source. Where the trading is on a regulated market it is a criminal offence under Pt V of the Criminal Justice Act 1993, subject to certain defences.

- Market abuse is a wider concept that includes insider dealing, but also includes other ways of creating a false market in securities which are traded on a regulated market, such as share ramping schemes. There are criminal penalties under s 397 of the Financial Services and Markets Act 2000.

- The Financial Services and Markets Act 2000 also provides a regime of administrative penalties for market abuse.

- Both the Financial Services Authority and the government can investigate alleged cases of insider dealing and market abuse.

- The best method of prevention of insider dealing and market abuse is for the market regulator to compel rapid disclosure of information so that secrets are kept to a minimum.

Essential Cases

R v Butt (2006): the vice-president of an investment bank was successfully prosecuted for insider dealing in breach of Pt V of the Criminal Justice Act 1993 by using confidential information gained through his work, which related to keeping information about proposed takeover bids confidential, and received a jail sentence.

R v Rigby (2006): the Chairman and Chief Executive (Rigby) and Chief Finance Officer (Bailey) of a listed company issued a misleading statement falsely suggesting that the company had already entered into certain contracts, which caused the share price to rise, following which it had to issue corrective statements and the share price fell dramatically. Although Rigby and Bailey did not deal in securities, they were convicted under s 397(1) of the Financial Services and Markets Act 2000 and sentenced to a term of imprisonment, a confiscation order and Rigby was disqualified as a director, the confiscation order being varied on appeal.

Davidson and Tatham v Financial Services Authority (2006): when faced with an accusation of market abuse under the administrative penalties regime, the standard of proof is on the balance of probabilities (the civil standard) but the standard should be applied flexibly: where the consequences of the allegations are serious, as they were in this case, a high standard of evidence would have to be reached to prove the case. In this case both Davidson and Tatham escaped liability.

Chase Manhattan Equities Ltd v Goodman (1991): where the director of a company, who owned a substantial shareholding, gifted the shares to his girlfriend, who then sold them just before the news broke that he had resigned as chairman, the recipient of the shares in the market transaction successfully sued the director in a civil action on the grounds that the contract was tainted with illegality because of the insider dealing, and therefore the contract was unenforceable.

18 THE COMPANY SECRETARY AND THE AUDITOR

Chapter 8 dealt with the most important of the company's officers: the directors. This chapter deals with two other office holders: the company secretary and the auditor.

THE COMPANY SECRETARY

A public company must have a company secretary under s 271 of the Companies Act 2006, although it is no longer necessary for a private company to do so. Many private companies will continue to have a secretary if they find the appointment useful. Like a director, a secretary is an officer of the company.

Functions of the secretary

What the secretary of a particular company does will depend on the size and scale of the particular company and how the work is organised. Even though a public company must appoint a company secretary, the Companies Act 2006 does not prescribe any particular duties. However, generally the secretary is the chief administrative officer within the company, and is not concerned with strategic management. The secretary is often responsible for filing the annual accounts and the annual returns and other notices to Companies House, and for maintaining the statutory registers, such as the register of members. The secretary will generally organise board meetings and general meetings and set agendas for these meetings in conjunction with the chairman.

Qualifications of the secretary

In contrast to directors, who do not need any academic qualifications, there are some requirements for the secretary of a public company to hold qualifications (s 273). The directors must take all reasonable steps to secure that the secretary has the knowledge and experience to discharge the functions required of him and possesses one of a range of formal qualifications such as membership of the Institute of Chartered Accountants of Scotland, the Association of Chartered Certified Accountants, the Institute of Chartered Secretaries and Administrators, the Chartered Institute of Management Accountants, or the Chartered Institute of Public Finance and Accountancy. Being a solicitor or advocate are also acceptable qualifications for a company secretary. Membership of other bodies that are not listed is also acceptable provided it appears to the directors that the person is capable of discharging the required functions.

Authority of the company secretary

As has been stated, the job description of any particular secretary ultimately comes from the board of directors. All the secretary's powers are delegated by the board. As an agent, the secretary would usually have to have express authority to do any act that binds the company. In *Barnett Hoares v South London Tramways Co* (1887) a secretary was held not to have authority to make representations on behalf of a company. However, nearly a century later, in *Panorama Developments (Guildford) Ltd v Fidelis Furnishing Fabrics Ltd* (1971) the court recognised that times had changed since *Barnett Hoares* was decided and in certain circumstances a company secretary could have apparent authority to make contracts and bind the company in a contract relating to the administrative side of a company's business, even where the directors did not approve the contract and did not want to honour it.

THE AUDITOR

Unless a company is exempt from having to have an audit, every company's annual accounts must be audited (s 475). These exemptions will be considered at the end of this chapter. By s 495, the purpose of the audit is to check that the accounts have been properly prepared in accordance with the relevant accounting framework and the Companies Act 2006 and that they show a true and fair view, in the case of the balance sheet, of the state of affairs of the company at the end of the financial year, and, in the case of the profit and loss account, of the profit or loss of the company for the financial year. The auditor has to report on the directors' report as to whether in his opinion the information in the directors' report is consistent with the annual accounts (s 496). If the auditor is not able to reconcile statements in the accounts with the underlying books and records, the report must be qualified. In a quoted company, the auditor must also report on the auditable part of the directors' remuneration report, by s 497.

It must be remembered that the members of a company do not have access to the company's books or its management accounts, and they are therefore unable to watch over the directors' stewardship of the company's affairs very effectively. They are reliant on what the directors tell them. The auditor, by contrast, has various rights to obtain the necessary information to be an effective watchdog for the members.

Qualifications

Like the secretary of a public company, the auditor has to hold formal qualifications. It is a requirement under European Union Directive 2006/43/EC that an auditor must be subject to public oversight. This can be by a professional body of which the auditor is a member, provided that the professional body is itself subject to public oversight. In the UK, this function is carried out by the Professional Oversight Board of the Financial Reporting Council (see www.frc.org.uk/pob/). By s 1212 of the Companies Act 2006, to act as auditor, an individual or firm must be (a) a member of a recognised supervisory body and (b) authorised for appointment under the rules of that body.

An auditor needs to have a qualification recognised by the Public Oversight Board. Membership of those UK accounting professional bodies where auditing is part of the qualification, such as the Institute of Chartered Accountants of Scotland or the Association of Chartered Certified Accountants would be appropriate routes to a career as an auditor.

An auditor also needs to be a fit and proper person to act as an auditor under Sch 10, para 8 to the Companies Act 2006, and, by s 1214, the auditor must be independent of the company. A person would not be independent if he was an officer or employee of the company which is the subject of the audit, or a partner or employee of such a person.

The appointment of the auditor

A company must usually appoint an auditor under ss 485 (private companies) and 489 (public companies), unless the directors reasonably resolve otherwise on the grounds that audited accounts are unlikely to be required. The first auditors must be appointed before the date of the first accounts meeting. Usually an auditor is appointed annually in a public company and holds office until the end of the next annual general meeting, when he is generally reappointed for a further year by ordinary resolution. In a private company (by s 487), the auditor is usually deemed to be reappointed each year automatically unless another auditor is appointed, except where the auditor was appointed by the directors, or the Articles call for actual reappointment, or the members prevent reappointment by submitting notice to the company supported by the holders of at least 5 per cent of the voting rights (s 488), or the members have resolved not to reappoint, or the directors have resolved not to appoint an auditor for that financial year. The directors also have power to fill a casual vacancy in the office of auditor, and the members can do so by ordinary resolution if the directors do not. The Secretary of State for Business, Innovation and Skills has default powers to appoint an auditor where the company has not done so, under ss 486 and 490 for private and public companies respectively.

The legal position of the auditor

Part 16 of the Companies Act 2006 refers to the "office" of auditor in ss 487 and 491, although the auditor is not defined as an "officer of the company" by s 1261. Section 492 provides that: where the auditor was appointed by the members, the auditor's remuneration must be fixed by them by ordinary resolution; where the auditor was appointed by the directors, the remuneration must be fixed by the directors; and, where the auditor was appointed by the Secretary of State, the remuneration must be fixed by him.

The duties and rights of the auditor

The task of the auditor under s 498 is to investigate in order to form an opinion on:

- whether adequate accounting records have been kept and adequate returns have been made from branches the auditor did not visit, on which to base the audit;
- whether the accounts are in agreement with the accounting records;
- in a quoted company, whether the auditable part of the directors' remuneration report is in agreement with the accounting records and returns;
- in a public company whose securities are listed, in relation to which the accounts must include a corporate governance statement, whether the statement has been prepared (s 498A).

If the auditor is not satisfied with the adequacy on any of these, or where they are missing, this must be stated in the auditor's report. The same applies where the auditor considers that the information and explanations provided by the company are inadequate, and where the auditor considers that the disclosure requirements on directors' remuneration and benefits and, in a quoted company, on the remuneration report have not been complied with.

The information rights and rights of audience of the auditor

If the auditor is to be an effective watchdog for the members' interests, he must be able to get beyond relying solely on information provided by the directors. After all, the directors may have perpetrated a fraud which they have done their best to conceal, and which they are hoping the auditor will not uncover. For this reason, the auditor is given various rights to obtain information by ss 499–501, as follows:

- the right of access at all times to the company's books, accounts and vouchers in whatever form they are held (backed by criminal penalties for non-compliance);
- the right to call for information or an explanation from officers of the company, employees, and persons holding company books and vouchers, and from its subsidiaries including overseas subsidiaries (backed by criminal penalties);
- the right under s 502(1) and (2) to receive notice of all general meetings of the company and, in the case of a private company, to receive a copy of all written resolutions;
- the right to speak at any general meeting of the company on any part of the business of the meeting that concerns him as auditor (s 502(3));
- after ceasing office, an auditor who has been removed has the right to attend a general meeting at which his office would have expired, or which has been called to fill a casual vacancy, and take part in the part of the meeting that concerns him as former auditor (s 513). Similar provisions apply to a resigning auditor under s 518.

Removal, resignation and replacement of the auditor

Again, in order to ensure that it is hard for the directors to persuade an auditor to stop probing and to "go quietly", there are statutory rules to ensure that, where an auditor ceases office, there is an opportunity to blow the whistle and inform the members where appropriate.

Removal

The procedure for removal of an auditor is similar to the procedure for removal of a director. Section 510 provides that an auditor may be removed from office at any time by the members by ordinary resolution. Special notice (28 days' advance notice to the company) is required. Notice of the meeting must be given to the members and to the auditor. The auditor is entitled under s 511 to require the company to send out to the members, in advance of the meeting, his written representations (of reasonable length) stating his position. The auditor also has the right to speak at the meeting. The auditor may also be entitled to compensation for loss of office. As a result of this right to be heard, a private company may not remove an auditor by written ordinary resolution under s 288. Companies House must be notified within 14 days.

As mentioned above, an auditor who has been removed may return to haunt the company, in that he has the right to attend a general meeting at which his term of office was due to expire, or which has been called to fill a casual vacancy, and take part in any business at that meeting that concerns him as former auditor (s 518).

An auditor of a company who ceases for any reason to hold office must under s 519 deposit at the company's registered office a statement as to whether there are circumstances related to the company that led him to cease office, which need to be drawn to the attention of the members or creditors. If the company is not a quoted company, the auditor is allowed to deposit a statement to the effect that there are no such circumstances. This provision is backed by criminal penalties. If the notice discloses that there are circumstances related to the company which need to be drawn to the attention of the members or creditors, the company must then send a copy of the statement to all persons who are entitled to receive copies of the accounts, or apply to the court to be excused (s 520). Again, this provision is backed by criminal penalties.

By s 522, the auditor has duties to notify an appropriate audit authority where he has left office for any reason, in cases where the audit is a "major audit" (an audit of a listed company or a company in which there is major public interest). If the audit does not class as a major audit, notification is only needed where the auditor ceases to hold office before the expiration of his term of office. The *company* also has to notify the appropriate audit authority under s 523 when an auditor has ceased office before the expiration of his term of office, sending a copy of the auditor's statement of reasons for leaving office and the company's own explanation of events.

Further reporting of these events is necessary: when it receives this information, the audit authority must (under s 524) inform the accounting authorities, namely the Secretary of State for Business, Innovation and Skills and, currently, the Financial Reporting Review Panel.

When an auditor has been removed from office on the grounds of divergence of opinion on accounting treatments or audit procedures or on any other improper grounds, that can give rise to a petition by a member or members seeking a remedy on the grounds of unfairly prejudicial conduct under s 994(1A) of the Companies Act 2006, which was referred to in Chapter 11.

Resignation

An auditor may resign from office at any time by sending written notice to the company's registered office under s 516. Again, Companies House must be informed within 14 days.

It may be that an auditor is resigning not for personal reasons, but because of something to do with the company. The Companies Act 2006, by s 518 gives the auditor rights in order to ensure that the auditor can explain the circumstances to the members, where appropriate.

An auditor who is resigning before the expiration of his term of office can, under s 518, give a signed requisition along with his written resignation to the directors, demanding that they immediately convene an extraordinary general meeting to discuss the circumstances with the members, and can demand that his written representations of reasonable length be sent to the members in advance of the meeting, explaining his position. This right can be removed by court order if the court is satisfied that it is being abused. There is a time limit placed on the directors for convening this meeting and the provision is backed by criminal penalties. The auditor is entitled to speak at that meeting.

An auditor who is resigning has the same obligation under s 519 as an auditor who is being removed, to make a statement about reasons for ceasing office. This provision was explained above.

Replacement

When an auditor's appointment is not renewed, or the auditor does not seek reappointment, the auditor has the same obligation as a resigning auditor to notify the company, under s 519 as to whether there are circumstances related to the company that led him to cease office, which need to be drawn to the attention of the members or creditors.

Rights of members of a quoted company to require website publication of audit concerns

Section 527 allows the members of a quoted company who together hold at least 5 per cent of the total voting rights or 100 members together holding shares on which an average of £100 per member has been paid up to give notice to the company requiring it to publish on its website a statement about concerns they have about the audit of the accounts or the circumstances in which the auditor ceased office that they wish to raise at the next accounts meeting. The company has a right to obtain a court order to prevent publication if it can convince the court that the right is being abused. The provision is backed by criminal penalties.

Liability of the auditor

Liability to the company

The auditor has a contract with the company. If the company has issues with the auditor about the quality of the audit, it can sue the auditor for breach of contract. The company can also sue the auditor in the law of delict, as the auditor does owe a duty of care to the company, since the auditor is fully aware that the company will rely on its audited accounts in its decision-making and therefore has the necessary relationship of proximity. The courts, over many years, have defined the standard of care that the auditor must show towards the company whose accounts are audited. In *Re Kingston Cotton Mill Co (No 2)* (1896) Lopes LJ famously stated that the auditor is a "watchdog, but not a bloodhound" and does not guarantee that all fraud would be discovered. It was held in *Barings plc v Coopers and Lybrand* (1997) that a company might reasonably expect an auditor to identify weaknesses in internal controls and make it probable that material misstatements would be brought to light. In *Stone & Rolls Ltd (in Liquidation) v Moore Stephens* (2009), in which the auditor was sued by the liquidator of a company for failing to uncover a fraud on various banks perpetrated by a person who was shadow director and sole beneficial shareholder of a company, it was held by the House of Lords that the auditor was allowed to defend itself by arguing that an action could not be raised by the company in contract and tort (delict in Scotland) because no right of action can arise from an illegality (*ex turpi causa non oritur actio*) and the fraud had to be regarded in these circumstances as having been committed by the company itself.

Liability to other persons

Actions for negligence against the auditors have often been raised by persons other than the company where they have suffered loss caused by relying on accounts which they consider have been negligently audited. It was held by the House of Lords in *Caparo Industries plc v Dickman* (1990) that, where it is claimed that shareholders have suffered as a result of a negligent audit, the duty of care is owed to the *company* and not to individual shareholders who bought shares relying on the accuracy of the accounts and then suffered loss when the company became insolvent. The auditor lacked the necessary relationship of proximity to the shareholders. For an auditor to be liable, it is necessary to show that the auditor is or should be aware that the audited financial statements are likely to be relied on by a person who is identifiable in some way by the auditor. See also *Royal Bank of Scotland plc v Bannerman Johnstone Maclay* (2005).

However, outside parties have on occasion been able to establish delictual liability, if they can establish both the necessary causal link between the legal wrong and the loss (which was not achieved in *JEB Fasteners Ltd v Marks Bloom & Co* (1983)) and the necessary proximity. However, in cases where an auditor has a contract with a company to prepare a report in connection with a proposed sale of shares to another party, courts have recognised that there *can* be delictual liability towards the other party who then relies on the accuracy of that report and buys shares, only to suffer loss caused by negligence in the preparation of the report. An example of a case in which an action for negligence against an auditor was successful in connection with such a report is *ADT Ltd v BDO Binder Hamlyn* (1996).

Relief from liability

Until fairly recently, provisions in the Articles of Association or any contract with the company which would exclude or limit the auditor's liability for negligence, default, breach of duty or breach of trust in the course of auditing the accounts, or where the auditor is provided with an indemnity against liability, would always be void. The position now, under ss 532–538, is that while this is still the normal position, it is permissible for the company to grant the auditor an indemnity for the expenses of successfully defending himself in court in civil or criminal proceedings or where the auditor is relieved of liability by a court under s 1157. This kind of indemnity can also be granted to directors.

The other exception is where the auditor and the company have entered into a liability limitation agreement. These were introduced in the Companies Act 2006 because there had been cases where liability was imposed on auditors that exceeded the limit of their professional indemnity insurance. This was making audit firms reluctant to undertake large and complex audits, and led to the creation of the limited liability partnership described in Chapter 3. A liability limitation agreement has to be authorised by the members by ordinary resolution under s 536, although a private company can pass a resolution waiving the need for approval. Section 537 imposes restrictions on the extent of a liability limitation agreement: it must be fair and reasonable in all the circumstances of the case, having regard to the auditor's statutory responsibilities, the nature and purpose of the auditor's contractual obligations to the company, and the professional standards expected of the auditor. By s 536, it may apply to only one financial year and the contents of these agreements and an obligation of disclosure of the agreement in the accounts are regulated by subordinate legislation. It can also be withdrawn by ordinary resolution before the start of the financial year to which it relates. It must be disclosed in the annual accounts.

EXEMPTION FROM THE REQUIREMENT TO CARRY OUT AN AUDIT

Not every company is required to have its accounts audited. Although all public companies must appoint an auditor, as explained earlier in this chapter, some private companies are exempt from this requirement because they are small companies as defined in s 477, dormant companies as defined in s 480, or not-profit-making companies subject to public sector audit, as defined in s 482. These exemptions will now be explored.

Small companies

Under s 382, a small company is a company which satisfies two out of the following three requirements:

- its turnover in the particular financial year is not more than £6.5 million;
- its balance sheet total is not more than £3.26 million; and
- the number of employees is not more than 50.

With some exceptions, a small company may, if it wishes, file abbreviated accounts at Companies House, although full accounts must be presented to its members. Under s 477, a small company that satisfies the first two requirements above may be exempt from the requirement to have its accounts audited. It must make a statement to this effect in its balance sheet. The members may, however, insist on an audit being held, if members representing at least 10 per cent in nominal value of the company's issued share capital, or, if the company does not have a share capital, 10 per cent in number of the members give notice calling for an audit under s 476.

Dormant companies

This term applies to small private companies that are not carrying on business or are not in operation in a particular financial year. Again, there must be a statement in its balance sheet to the effect that the company is exempt from the requirement of an audit. Section 480 provides some conditions for claiming this exemption. Again, it is subject to the right of the members under s 476 to require an audit.

Public sector companies

These may be exempt from audit under ss 482–483 because they are subject to a public sector audit by a public official such as the Auditor General for Scotland.

Essential Facts

- A public company must appoint a company secretary, although this is optional for a private company.
- The secretary of a public company usually needs to hold professional qualifications.
- The tasks of the company secretary are delegated by the board of directors.
- A company secretary is the chief administrative officer of a company and may nowadays have apparent authority to bind the company in contracts relating to the administrative function, even if not expressly authorised by the directors.
- The accounts of all public companies and all except small private companies, dormant companies and certain public sector companies must be audited.
- The role of the auditor is to reconcile the financial accounts with the underlying books and accounts and certify that they

show a true and fair view of the company's financial position as at the balance sheet date and of its profit and loss in a particular financial year.

- An auditor has to hold a formal qualification in auditing, and must be subject to public oversight. The auditor must also be independent of the company.
- The auditor of a public company is appointed annually and holds office until the conclusion of the next accounts meeting. In a private company the appointment may roll over from year to year.
- Being an auditor is an "office".
- The auditor has statutory duties to reconcile the books and records of the company with the annual accounts. If the auditor is not satisfied, the auditor's report must be qualified.
- The auditor has various information rights to ensure he is not fobbed off by the directors, and rights to attend and participate in general meetings of the company.
- The members of a company can remove an auditor by ordinary resolution on special notice, although the auditor has the right to make written or oral representations to the members.
- Auditors who cease office have a duty to make a statement relating to any reasons for ceasing office which relate to the company. These must be drawn to the attention of members and creditors, and in some cases the audit authority.
- A resigning auditor can requisition the directors to convene an extraordinary general meeting.
- In a quoted company, the members have certain rights to have their concerns relating to the audit published on the company's website to put it on notice that they will raise these concerns at the next accounts meeting.
- An auditor will be liable at common law to the company in contract if it fails to carry out the audit as required under the contract.
- An auditor may also be liable to the company at common law for negligence relating to the audit.
- Generally, the auditor is not liable to parties other than the company for negligence, but may be liable where a relationship of proximity between the auditor and the outside party can be established.

• Generally, the auditor may not contract out of liability but may be relieved of liability for the expenses of successfully defending himself in civil or criminal proceedings, and may in some circumstances make a liability limitation agreement with the company.

Essential Cases

Barnett Hoares v South London Tramways Co (1887): the secretary of the tramway company was asked for information by a bank that was going to lend to one of the tramway company's contractors, as to how much money was still to be paid by the tramway company to the contractor. The secretary overstated the amount owed. When the contractors defaulted on the bank loan, the bank sought to make the tramway company liable. The court held that a company secretary had no authority to make representations on behalf of the company, as a secretary was, in the words of Lord Esher, a "mere servant; his position is to do what he is told".

Panorama Developments (Guildford) Ltd v Fidelis Furnishing Fabrics Ltd (1971): a secretary who hired Jaguars and Rolls Royces in the name of the company, but without express authority, could bind the company in the law of agency by apparent authority, as the contract related to the administrative side of the company's affairs. The dicta of Lord Esher in *Barnett Hoares* were held no longer to be applicable.

Re Kingston Cotton Mill (No 2) (1896): in a company where the audited accounts were based on fraudulent valuations of stock, on which dividends had wrongly been paid, despite the fact that the auditor could have found out the true position if the stock had been checked, there was held to be no duty on an auditor to take stock and, in the absence of grounds for suspicion, the auditor could rely on the certificates of a manager who was also one of the directors.

Barings plc v Coopers and Lybrand (1997): where the auditor of a subsidiary company had failed to detect fraud, there was an arguable case that a parent company might be owed a duty of care by the auditor of the subsidiary.

Stone & Rolls Ltd (in Liquidation) v Moore Stephens (2009): where a company sued its auditors for negligence for failing to detect fraud, the action was not competent because the defence that no right of action can be founded on an illegality could be argued by the auditor as a defence (*ex turpi causa non oritur actio*) where the fraud was perpetrated by a shadow director who was the sole beneficial shareholder of a company. In these circumstances, the fraud was considered to be the act of the company.

Caparo Industries plc v Dickman (1990): an auditor who fails to detect irregularities in the accounts on which decisions were taken to purchase shares in a company which subsequently went into liquidation, does not owe a duty of care to persons who bought shares relying on the truth of the accounts, because they cannot establish the required relationship of proximity. It made no difference whether or not they already held shares before making their purchase. For the auditor to be liable in these circumstances, it would have to be proved that the auditor knew that a statement would be communicated to an identifiable party who would be likely to rely on it. Any duty of care in these circumstances is owed to the company, ie to the shareholders as a body.

Royal Bank of Scotland plc v Bannerman Johnstone Maclay (2005): An auditor might potentially be liable to a bank that lent money on the basis of audited accounts, which were claimed to be negligently audited, where the company's business plan was prepared by the audit firm and a member of the audit firm had been seconded to the company. In such a case there might be a duty of care in these circumstances even if the firm did not intend that the third party (the bank) should rely on its statements.

JEB Fasteners Ltd v Marks Bloom & Co (1983): where negligently audited accounts were relied on as the basis for a take-over bid, there could be no right of action where the company had discovered the inaccuracy in the accounts for themselves and went ahead with the takeover anyway. In such a case, the necessary element of causation is missing.

ADT Ltd v BDO Binder Hamlyn (1996): where an auditor was specifically questioned about the accounts just prior to a takeover bid, and the auditor was aware of the purpose of the meeting and that the answers would be relied on in making a bid, the necessary relationship of proximity would be present, to make an auditor liable in negligence, and in this case liability of £65 million was imposed on the auditor.

19 INSTITUTIONAL FRAMEWORK OF COMPANIES

As has been seen throughout this book, various bodies are responsible for the regulation of companies. In this chapter, the two most important will be discussed: the Department for Business, Innovation and Skills (which is the UK government department responsible for the regulation of companies) and Companies House (which is responsible for their registration). It must be remembered that there are various other bodies which may concern themselves with the affairs of companies, such as the Financial Services Authority (discussed in Chapter 17) and the Competition Commission and Office of Fair Trading, which may concern themselves with companies when there are issues such as mergers that may affect the market. As was seen in Chapter 17, the government department responsible for financial regulation is HM Treasury.

In this chapter, the work of the Department for Business, Innovation and Skills and of Companies House will be briefly reviewed, as being of particular relevance in the regulation of the affairs of companies.

THE DEPARTMENT FOR BUSINESS, INNOVATION AND SKILLS (BIS)

Company law is not a devolved matter, and legislation is enacted by the UK Parliament. Some aspects of corporate insolvency law are currently devolved to the Scottish Parliament. The Department for Business, Innovation and Skills is the UK department responsible for company law. It was this department (under a previous name) that decided, soon after the previous Labour Government came into power in 1997, to undertake a radical review of company legislation, with a view to modernising it and where possible simplifying it. This resulted in the Companies Act 2006, which is now almost completely in force.

Some initiatives for corporate legislation come from the BIS itself, whereas many provisions originate with the European Union, largely in the form of Directives. In these cases there may be relatively little choice in the content of the legislation, which then has to be passed by Parliament or passed by BIS by subordinate legislation, although the UK participates along with the representatives of the other Member States in drafting and approving the Directives.

Much of company law takes the form of subordinate legislation made by BIS.

The most relevant part of the BIS website appears on the pages on company and partnership law, which are available at www.bis.gov.uk/policies/business-law/company-and-partnership-law.

The BIS has powers over companies which it can exercise in the public interest (these have been referred to in various places throughout this book). They include the powers to investigate the affairs of companies which are currently still found in the old Companies Act 1985, in ss 431–457. These allow the BIS in certain circumstances to appoint inspectors, to call for the production of documents, to enter and search premises, and to impose restrictions on the rights attaching to shares to assist an investigation.

The BIS can also seek to wind up companies on the "just and equitable" ground for the public interest, following an investigation, by seeking a court order under s 124A of the Insolvency Act 1986 where it considers that the company's affairs have been conducted in a manner that is unfairly prejudicial to the interests of the members generally or some part of the members, seeking a remedy. This was discussed in Chapter 11.

In relation to directors of companies in insolvent liquidation, the BIS can seek to have these directors disqualified on the grounds that their conduct shows them to be unfit to take part in the management of a company in terms of s 6 of the Company Directors Disqualification Act 1986. This is either done by court order or by the Department offering the director a chance to give an undertaking not to act as a director for a period of years. If the evidence is established, the court must disqualify the director, and the time period of the disqualification is from 2 to 15 years.

At the time of writing, the Scotland Bill to devolve new powers to the Scottish Parliament has been published and has had its Second Reading in the UK Parliament. This proposes to reserve power to legislate in corporate insolvency to the UK Parliament, and, if this is enacted, it would give the BIS new powers in this area.

COMPANIES HOUSE

Companies House is an executive agency of the BIS. It is responsible for the registration of companies and this function has existed in the UK since 1844. Companies House incorporates new companies by registering them and granting them certificates of incorporation, granting them legal personality, and at the end of their corporate life it dissolves them.

It also registers a great deal of mandatory information about companies, that members, creditors and others may find useful to know about, such as the annual accounts, annual returns (showing who the directors and members are and key legal events during the year such as a new share issue), or the granting of a security for a loan. Some of this information is freely available to the public by using the Companies House Webcheck service, while other information is available for a small fee.

Companies House is organised regionally, with the main office in Cardiff being responsible for companies in England and Wales, an office in Edinburgh registering Scottish companies, and another in Belfast for Northern Irish companies.

Companies House has a website (www.companieshouse.gov.uk) that holds a wealth of useful information for those who run companies. It also provides access to the Register of Companies, to check what companies are currently registered, and to the register of disqualified directors.

INDEX

NOTES

NOTES

NOTES

NOTES

NOTES

NOTES

NOTES